MUSEUMS INVOLVING COMMUNITIES

Museums Involving Communities: Authentic Connections explores how museums can become more active and also considers how they might involve members of their local communities in their everyday work.

Examining the key components of the museum–community relationship, this book looks at both the impact of museums on the cultural and civic lives of local communities and the impact of local communities on the programs, collections, and organizational culture of museums. Advocating an accessible and inclusive approach to museum management, Kadoyama focuses on the role of museum leadership in fostering and deepening community relationships. The result offers insights into how relationships between communities and museums can be forged in practice, how museums can be involved in building healthier communities, and how community engagement strategies can be developed, implemented, and evaluated successfully.

Written by an experienced museum professional with extensive experience in community involvement and audience development, *Museums Involving Communities* is key reading for museum workers looking to make an impact, while building long-term relations with local communities, to the benefit of both museum and community. It should also be of great interest to students taking courses in museum and heritage studies.

Margaret Kadoyama has over thirty-five years of experience in the museum profession. She is a faculty member at John F. Kennedy University, USA, and principal of Margaret Kadoyama Consulting, a consultancy specializing in community engagement and audience development.

MUSEUMS INVOLVING COMMUNITIES

Authentic Connections

Margaret Kadoyama

Routledge
Taylor & Francis Group

NEW YORK AND LONDON

First published 2018
by Routledge
711 Third Avenue, New York, NY 10017

and by Routledge
2 Park Square, Milton Park, Abingdon, Oxon, OX14 4RN

Routledge is an imprint of the Taylor & Francis Group, an informa business

© 2018 Taylor & Francis

Library of Congress Cataloging-in-Publication Data
A catalog record for this book has been requested

ISBN: 978-0-8153-8459-5 (hbk)
ISBN: 978-1-62958-494-2 (pbk)
ISBN: 978-1-351-20399-9 (ebk)

Typeset in Bembo
by Keystroke, Neville Lodge, Tettenhall, Wolverhampton

Printed in the United Kingdom
by Henry Ling Limited

CONTENTS

PART III
Challenges, Outcomes, Impacts, and Accountability   **133**

ILLUSTRATIONS

Figures

Boxes

PREFACE

This book is the result of a long commitment to teaching and the quiet but tenacious goal of helping people learn how museums can be vital members of their communities. Since the late 1980s I have been committed to this vision, and when I was asked to teach at John F. Kennedy University Museum Studies in 1997, I hoped that this was a way to influence many students over many years to embrace and incorporate community involvement into their daily practice. It has been a great pleasure to see hundreds of JFKU students embracing community work and joining with colleagues in moving this forward. To my delight, the museum field has grown and is increasingly embracing community-focused work.

The seed for this book came from a simple question. Mitch Allen, Left Coast Press's publisher, asked me, "When are you going to write a book for me? You can use your course syllabus as your guide." Mitch's clear and simple suggestion provided the spark. My twenty years of teaching Museums and Communities at JFKU has provided a considerable amount of content, and my students and their work have inspired this book. The course was the launching point for organizing and considering what to include and what new insights shine a light on this work. Later that year, when Left Coast Press retired and the book came under the purview of Routledge, I had the good fortune to work with Routledge's team.

This book results from years of being a practitioner and teacher, focusing on museums and cultural organizations being involved with their communities. I launched my work with JFKU in 1997, when Marjorie Schwarzer, then chair of the department, invited me to teach the Museums and Diversity course. I changed it slightly, to focus on how I like to describe the work: Museums and Diverse Communities.

In writing a book that is based on the value of inclusion, the question of what to include and what not to include was a constant consideration. A great number of people in many fields – people skilled in community activism, planners, practitioners, museum leaders, and foundations – focus on inclusion and community involvement. This book includes those contributions that provide the most interesting perspective to illustrate specific elements. As a result, many important contributions are not included or highlighted.

At this time and place (the United States in 2017), colleagues in many museums and cultural organizations are articulating the importance of being inclusive. John Dichtl, president and CEO of the American Association for State and Local History, wrote in a letter to the field on November 21, 2016, "AASLH will strive for inclusivity and urge its members to be even better at telling the full range of stories about our collective past." Laura Lott, president and CEO of the American Alliance of Museums, wrote in a statement on the travel ban imposed by Executive Order in January 2017,

> The American Alliance of Museums strongly believes in active participation in the global community and in welcoming international perspectives. We seek out and embrace a diversity of people and cultures to enhance our understanding of the world and to connect museums in a global context, as outlined in the Alliance's strategic plan.

Lastly, as I was editing the first draft of this book, my colleague Leslie Bedford asked:

Why are some museums comfortable and successful at embracing community and others not? How is that culture of inclusion created and sustained?

This book hopes to help you find out.

Bibliography

Dichtl, J. (2016, November 21). Letter from the president: Moving on from election week [Blog post]. Retrieved from http://blogs.aaslh.org/letter-from-the-president-moving-on-from-election-week/#sthash.a5voHLpy.dpuf

Lott, L. (2017, January 30). American Alliance of Museums statement on the Travel Ban imposed January 27 via Executive Order [Press release]. Retrieved from http://www.aam-us.org/about-us/media-room/2017/american-alliance-of-museums-statement-on-the-travel-ban-imposed-january-27-via-executive-order/?utm_source=MagnetMail&utm_medium=Email&utm_campaign=Aviso%3A%20Your%20AAM%20Member%20Newsletter

ACKNOWLEDGMENTS

Writing acknowledgments is a wholehearted process, a way to thank and deeply acknowledge all those who have contributed to the creation of this book and those whose support has accompanied me on this path. These are my communities.

The students, alums, and faculty at John F. Kennedy University Museum Studies are always in my heart and mind. The students' work in the Museums and Communities course is a constant reminder of the beauty and complexity of museums connecting deeply with their communities. Their dedication, while they are students and when they are alums working in the field, continues to inspire me. The faculty of JFKU, especially Adrienne McGraw and Susan Spero, have long supported this vision of museums and communities, and I am deeply grateful for the opportunity to teach.

I am forever grateful to Mitch Allen, publisher of Left Coast Press, who instigated this book and has been so supportive over the years.

My communities, people who have welcomed me and walked with me, have been the backbone of my work for many years. Jeff Mori, Rev. Timothy Dupre, David Escobar, Cecilia Zamora, Vinh Luu, Kim Shuck, and Katherine Toy, I thank you.

I am grateful to Exhibit Envoy (formerly California Exhibition Resources Alliance), which has supported this approach for years. Specifically, I thank the group who worked with me on the *Sing Me Your Story, Dance Me Home: Art and Poetry from Native California* community connections project over three years. Funded through an IMLS grant, the SMYS project supported small museums as they connected with their local native communities, and advisors Paula Allen, Gerald Clarke, Theresa Harlan, Judith Lowry, Linda Noel, and Sherrie Smith-Ferri gave of themselves time and time again. Lisa Eriksen, Lexie Smith Kleibe, Joan Jasper, and Adrienne McGraw were supportive throughout.

The development of this book coincided with my participation on the Museums and Race team, and I am grateful for the perspectives this provided. I especially enjoyed learning from Brenda Tindal as we served on the planning team together; from steering committee members Porchia Moore, Gretchen Jennings, Mary Ellen Munley, and Daryl Fischer for their dedication to continue a vibrant conversation; and from my fellow steering committee members Omar Eaton-Martinez, Joanne Jones-Rizzi, and Gina Díaz for walking this path together.

The development of this book also coincided with my joining the Museum Group, and I have been honored to be able to converse with TMG colleagues over issues and questions of critical importance to the field. I am deeply grateful to my TMG colleagues for sharing their perspectives and insights on creating equitable institutions and working for social change as we strive for change in the field.

I am grateful to the people who shared their stories for this book, for their honesty and generosity in giving their time and attention. Cassie Chinn's, Devon Akmon's, Jeremy Liu's, Kelly McKinley's, Prerana Reddy's, Chris Siefert's, Jane Werner's, Deborah Schwartz's, Lorie Millward's, and Joanne Jones-Rizzi's stories are included here, and I thank them.

My great thanks go to good friends and esteemed colleagues Marsha Semmel, Gretchen Jennings, Joanne Jones-Rizzi, and Gail Anderson, who read draft chapters and sent insightful comments and suggestions. This book is better because of them! Extra thanks go to Gail Anderson, whose support over many years as a treasured friend and colleague has meant a great deal. Great thanks are due to Ariel Weintraub, whose careful and thoughtful edits were so instrumental in creating a seamless final draft.

My work has been inspired by so many whose specific words may not be reflected in these pages but whose spirit is. Elaine Heumann Gurian, Marjorie Schwarzer, Roy Eisenhardt, Lucy Matzger, Nina Simon, Randy Roberts, Ellen Hirzy, Ron Chew, and Lisa Sasaki, your support and actions are guiding lights.

And finally, my heartfelt appreciation goes to my family: To my mother and father, who instilled in me the value of community service and who have practiced it throughout their lives; to my in-laws, who welcomed me into the Nakamoto and Kadoyama families; and to my husband, Bob, and daughters, Hana and Marie, whose lifelong support and thoughtful, thought-provoking conversations about community, identity, inclusion, social justice, respect, racism, and so much more feed me daily. You have my deepest love and gratitude.

INTRODUCTION

The purpose of this book is to explore how museums can become vital members of their communities, actively involved in community revitalization, and how community members can become actively involved with their museums. This exploration examines the components of museum–community relationships, with the goal of creating more accessible, inclusive, and relevant museums and cultural organizations. This book will provide insights and guidance into how museums can be more fully engaged with their communities. It will also ask questions about communities' impacts on museum programs, exhibitions, collections, audiences and internal culture; a museum's impact on its community; and the role of leadership in fostering community engagement. This book will guide the readers to a) understand how relationships between communities and museums can be forged, b) learn and weigh strategies for involving and advocating for communities in museums, and c) learn how to develop a community involvement action plan.

Communities are not unilateral homogeneous entities but rather are composed of complex people. That complexity plays out in the relationships people have with one another, internally within the community and externally. Those complex relationships are at the core of how museums are involving their communities.

The themes of the American Alliance of Museum's annual meetings in recent years have been focused on museums as inclusive organizations: *The Social Value of Museums: Inspiring Change* in 2015 and *Gateways for Understanding: Diversity, Equity, Accessibility, and Inclusion in Museums* in 2017. In addition, this book highlights research that has been conducted over the past few years. These perspectives, from sociologists to community development professionals to communitarians and community builders, guide much of the understanding of effective practice in building healthier communities. Museum practitioners are hungry for more in-depth tools to assist them as they navigate this road. This book will provide those in-depth tools and will explore:

- How to learn about communities;
- Examples that illustrate this work, including descriptions of their practice. Examples will highlight the importance of tenacity and longevity in community involvement work, illustrating that the long-term impacts of this work might not be fully evident until a number of years have passed;
- What the readers can learn from the examples and what they can adapt for their own projects;
- How the readers can use their own research, including what they learn from the examples, to develop a plan to become more fully involved in their communities;
- Why community involvement is important, the core values that support it, and why it is important to look internally to understand oneself and one's organization;
- The tools to help implement museum–community involvement;
- The complexities of museums and communities;
- What community involvement means: How might it look? What does it feel like? What needs to happen for this community and this cultural organization to be involved with one another?

That's a big order and a daunting task, but the readers will learn a lot about themselves in the process. Much of the material in this book will push the readers into thinking and acting in ways that may be challenging, that are just a bit (or maybe more than a bit) uncomfortable. It is when we challenge ourselves to learn and do things differently that our perspective shifts, as well as our practice.

This book focuses on those tasks and on the big picture to help the readers understand the complexities of communities and their relationships with museums. The readers will continually think about what it means – how it might look, what it feels like, and what needs to happen for this community and this museum to be involved with one another. This book focuses on the elements that are necessary to create and sustain successful museum–community connections: being aware of one's own perceptions of various communities, learning about the concerns and interests of various communities, truly valuing diverse perspectives, and questioning one's own assumptions.

Part I focuses on the theory about communities, critical components of building healthier communities, and connecting museums to communities. It is intended to broaden and deepen the readers' understanding about what it takes to make museums vital members of their communities so they can take this approach into their own professional work. In Part II, the readers learn about the elements of a healthy, ongoing relationship among diverse communities and museums, and they learn about themselves. They will also learn about a community and develop a long-range plan for community involvement. Part III focuses on the challenges, outcomes, and impacts of cultural organizations being involved with their communities. A bibliography is included at the end of each chapter for the readers to learn more.

The examples are stories from the field, often in the form of interviews, because the voices of those involved resonate more than third-parties' voices. These stories are not like what one usually hears at conferences, which are often a list of programs and projects (i.e., this is what we did and here are some images that show it). The stories are not only about what someone did but also about why they did it, the challenges they met, how they navigated through those challenges, and the short-term and longer-term impacts of their work for the individuals, the museums, and the people and organizations in their communities.

Bibliography

Bergeron, A., & Tuttle, B. (2013). *Magnetic: The art and science of engagement*. Washington, DC: AAM Press.

Harlow, B. (2014). *The road to results: Effective practices for building arts audiences*. New York: The Wallace Foundation.

The Harwood Institute for Public Innovation. (n.d.). Our approach: Turning outward. Retrieved from http://theharwoodinstitute.org/overview/

The James Irvine Foundation. (n.d.a). Arts engagement: Strengthening the practice, supporting the field. Retrieved from https://www.irvine.org/arts

The James Irvine Foundation. (n.d.b). Arts engagement: Strengthening grantees. Retrieved from https://www.irvine.org/arts/who-we-fund

Partners for Livable Communities. (2011). *Culture connects all: Rethinking audiences in times of demographic change*. Retrieved from http://livable.org/livability-resources/reports-a-publications/520-culture-connects-all-

Partners for Livable Communities. (2012). *Stories for change*. Retrieved from http://livable.org/livability-resources/reports-a-publications/564-stories-for-change-

PART I

Community

First, we need to define community in broad terms. These broad terms include the relevant theories, learnings from other sectors, and a knowledge of how the philanthropic community defines this work. We look at the critical components of building healthier communities and consider what it takes to connect museums with their communities.

Within one's organization, as well as when one is connecting with community members, it is important to make sure that everyone agrees on terminology and expectations. Individuals may have different ways of thinking and talking about communities, and it is important to talk about and clarify what everyone means when they talk about "community."

Chapter 1 focuses on defining relevant terms, Chapter 2 expands on and delves deeper into building healthier communities and community well-being, and Chapter 3 explores the theory behind many of these definitions. In Chapters 4 and 5, the lens shifts to looking at the recent history of community-focused work in museums, followed by a look at how other community-focused fields inform museum practice.

It is important to clarify at the outset that the premise of this book is on museums being involved with their communities, with the acknowledgment that community members may not be part of the museum's current audiences. Community is very broadly defined in this book; it does not mean underserved community. Readers will be guided through a process of identifying the priority communities with whom they want a stronger relationship, where they can address strategic questions and articulate the reasons to focus on that specific community. When this process happens, *priority community* has a more specific definition.

Community involvement and *community immersion* are the preferred terms in this book. They capture the essence of the emotional impact of being involved. The sense of heartfelt connection is core to this work. When one is involved with something or someone, what does it feel like? How much time and energy does one spend thinking about that something that they are involved with? What would it be like if each museum leader and staff member committed time, energy, brainpower, and heart power to working in their community? What would it be like if community members committed time, energy, brainpower, and heart power to working with the organization? When one is involved, one is immersed.

1
DEFINING TERMS

There are many words and phrases used when describing community-focused work, and it is important to clarify what we mean when they are used.

Community

Belonging is a core aspect that will be explored throughout this book. When people come together and feel a sense of community, they feel included. That is at the core of community involvement. To understand the way *community* is used in the context of building healthier communities and connecting more fully with one's community, it is useful to turn to authors, psychologists, and scholars who have considered and researched the key attributes. Peter Block, writing in *Community: The Structure of Belonging*, illuminates some of the core aspects of community:

> *Community* as used here is about the experience of belonging. We are in community each time we find a place where we belong.
>
> *Block, 2008, p. xii*

Mark K. Smith (n.d.), writing in the *Encyclopedia of Informal Education*, describes three ways of expressing community:

- Community as a *place* – a neighborhood, for instance, or some other geographic definer;
- Community of *interest* – people come together for some reason other than place, where they share a common interest, identity, etc.;
- Community as *communion* – the feeling of community, of people coming together, with a sense of belonging.

These three lenses through which to understand community – place, interest, and sense of belonging – will be in play throughout this book. Some of the stories and examples will illustrate community projects that are geographically centered or place based, and some will illustrate how a community of interest is the impetus for the work. In all the stories, the importance of *connecting through relationships* illustrates how people come together and create a sense of belonging.

Community Assets

Using an *asset-based model* is effective when one is considering communities. Communities already have assets and capacities that can be useful in addressing community concerns. This contrasts with a needs-based model, which considers communities to be *in need* and does not readily acknowledge the assets and capacities that already exist within a community. This aligns with the understandings and core values that underpin this book – that people and communities are worthy of respect; that they have capacity and value; that they already have great stores of knowledge and understanding; and that it is one's responsibility to learn so one can better understand oneself, one's organization, and one's communities and work together to build healthier communities. Stories throughout this book illustrate several organizations and foundations that support and are engaged in this asset-based process. As John P. Kretzmann and John L. McKnight (1993) note in *Building Communities From the Inside Out*, "[Creative neighborhood leaders] are discovering that wherever there are effective community development efforts, those efforts are based upon an understanding, or map, of the community's assets, capacities and abilities" (pp. 5–6).

Social Capital

Robert Putnam (2000), writing in *Bowling Alone*, brought the idea of social capital to the mainstream. Social capital refers to networks – people's connections with one another – and how these connections have *value*. If one considers that physical capital is defined by physical objects and human capital is defined by the capacities individual people have, social capital is described as how people connect and their relationships with one another. Putnam has extensively researched people's relationships and connections, and he identified two dimensions of social capital that have relevance to the work with museums and communities: *bridging*, or outward-looking connections, and *bonding*, or inward-looking connections. Bridging is what people do when they connect with others who are new to them, when they say, "We're interested in having a stronger connection with the neighborhood right around us, and we currently don't really serve them." Bonding is when people say, "We're interested in strengthening relationships with our members. They are already a part of what we do, but we want to make sure we serve their needs to the best of our ability." Putnam notes that bridging is inclusive and bonding is exclusive, so it is important to understand the potential outcomes when each of these strategies is used. When a museum focuses on bridging, will current constituencies feel disregarded and not valued? When it focuses on bonding, will potential new relationships languish because the people feel that they don't matter? These considerations will help inform museum practice as one moves forward.

Public Capital

Public capital is a concept related to social capital and was developed by the Harwood Institute for Public Innovation. The Harwood Group conducted extensive research and wrote many reports on growing community strength in the 1990s. Its research describes the structures and relationships needed for communities to thrive:

> The Harwood Group's research and projects in communities across America suggests that for a community to work effectively, there is a set of fundamental structures, relationships, networks and norms that need to be in place. Public Capital is what we call this rich, dynamic, complex system. There are mini factors that we have identified along with the conditions and characteristics that make each one work. By uncovering and gauging a community's public capital, we can identify in which Stage of Community Life a community sits. And we can begin to think strategically about how to grow a community and what it will take.
>
> *The Harwood Group, 1999, p. 6*

The Harwood Group has identified nine factors of public capital:

> The tangible dimensions (an abundance of social gatherings, organized spaces for interaction, catalytic organizations, and safe havens for decision makers), the links between the tangible dimensions (strong, diverse leadership, informal networks and links, and conscious community discussion), and the underlying conditions of public capital (community norms for public life, and a shared purpose for the community).
>
> *The Harwood Group, 1999, p. 34*

Associational Life

Communities are built and maintained by people doing things together. Kretzmann and McKnight (1993) describe associational life in their book *Building Communities From the Inside Out*. An association is a group of people working together in formal or informal ways, some with elected officers and paid members, and some very loosely organized. In their words, "Associations, together with the capacities of individuals, are the basic community-building tools of local neighborhoods" (pp. 109–110).

Community Engagement

Community engagement has various meanings. According to the American Alliance of Museums (AAM), the Community Engagement Assessment:

> Assesses the museum's understanding of and relationship with its various communities and the communities' perception of and experience with the museum. It helps museums gather better input from their constituents, develop a more nuanced view about the community's demographics and needs, respond to the changing nature of its audiences and incorporate these findings into planning and operational decisions.
>
> *AAM, n.d.*

Kelly Ann Beavers and Kimberley Hodgson, writing for the American Planning Association, note in *Arts and Culture Briefing Paper 04*, published in 2011, "Community engagement is the process of public participation and involvement that promotes relationship building through learning, action, and the expression of needs and values."

Other community engagement definitions include the following from Americans for the Arts:

> The arts community has tended to use *community engagement* to mean the deliberate and active ways arts organizations engage constituents and publics in order to align organizational goals, programs, and services with community interests and needs. Another meaning of community engagement relates to locating programs in community settings and collaborating with community partners to foster participation of targeted community members in arts and cultural programs and activities.
>
> *Animating Democracy, n.d.a*

With so many varying definitions, museum leadership and staff need to clarify what they mean and what community engagement looks like at their museum. Chapter 6 explores internal questions such as these more thoroughly.

Community Stakeholder

The term *community stakeholder* is often used to refer to community members who care about, have a strong interest in, are affected by, or have an effect on a project. Stakeholders are anyone who will be impacted by anything that goes on in a community. They could be individuals, community organizations, informal groups, civic organizations, government entities, businesses, fraternal organizations, people who work in service organizations, people whom others identify as community leaders, and many others. Someone may be a stakeholder in one circumstance but not in another. For instance, if a community park is going to be refurbished, community stakeholders may include caregivers, dog owners, dog walkers, runners, residents whose homes border the park, neighborhood watch advocates, law enforcement agencies, and community garden advocates.

Community Gatekeeper

At times, community stakeholders are referred to as *community gatekeepers*, and this term is sometimes used to identify individuals (stakeholders) who control access into a community. This may be formal access, when one needs to have official approval to proceed with a project, or informal, when one needs to connect with community members and finds that there is skepticism about the project and one's motives. It is helpful to recognize when gatekeepers are among the stakeholders. Some gatekeepers may take it upon themselves to control access to communities (and not necessarily because other community members have granted them this authority), and some may be given this authority because they are trusted by other community members.

Civic Engagement

Civic engagement is often used interchangeably with community engagement. It includes working with elected officials and public decision makers as well as people in the business community, civic organizations, and funding organizations. Americans for the Arts describes civic engagement in this way:

> Civic engagement refers to the many ways in which people participate in civic, community, and political life and, by doing so, express their engaged citizenship. From proactively becoming better informed to participating in public dialogue on issues, from volunteering to voting, from community organizing to political advocacy, the defining characteristic of active civic engagement is the commitment to participate and contribute to the improvement of one's community, neighborhood, and nation. Civic engagement may be either a measure or a means of social change, depending on the context and intent of efforts.
>
> *Animating Democracy, n.d.b*

Inclusion

Inclusion and *equity* are terms that are related to and impact the success of cultural organizations whose goal is to be deeply involved with their communities. This section focuses on *inclusion* and how an inclusive culture nourishes community involvement.

In *Valuing Diversity: The Case for Inclusive Museums*, the Museums Association (in the United Kingdom) defines inclusion in this way:

> Our definition of inclusion recognizes that people need to feel connected and engaged. Inclusion can be defined as a state of being and feeling valued,

respected and supported. Practicing inclusion is necessary for diversity initiatives to work effectively.

2016, p. 3

In *Global Diversity & Inclusion Benchmarks: Standards for Organizations Around the World*, from The Diversity Collegium, inclusion is defined as:

A dynamic state of operating in which diversity is leveraged to create a fair, healthy, and high-performing organization or community. An inclusive environment ensures equitable access to resources and opportunities for all. It also enables individuals and groups to feel safe, respected, engaged, motivated, and valued, for who they are and for their contributions toward organizational and societal goals.

O'Mara, Richter, et al., 2016, p. 1

This book encourages a core set of values, among them respect, empathy, and holding diverse perspectives and experiences in high regard. These core values are active throughout this book and are included in the examples from the field; these definitions; and all the following words, concepts, and suggested actions.

Characteristics of Community

This section examines selected characteristics and attributes of communities – ideas that are important to consider as one learns more about communities.

Complexity

Communities are complex. Communities are made up of people, and people are complex. Consider the various communities that you are part of: your neighborhood, the people you work with, the people you have fun with, people your kids/family members go to school with, the people you spend your time with in off-work hours, and the people in your faith community, book groups, etc. These groups come together in ways large and small. For each community, there is something that draws it together to become a community. To describe this community using just one characteristic would be too simplistic. Wherever there are people together in community, there are relationships, and relationships are complex.

At times, one may be tempted to describe communities in simplistic ways, using just one characteristic to call a group a community. If we expand the definition, it becomes clear that communities are complex and they are sometimes divided entities. Even within a small community, people have many perspectives, and it is important to recognize that there may be great differences in opinions. Within a single community, there may be people who are affluent, not so affluent, poor, old, young, and in between. A community may well encompass different ethnic groups with different – and sometimes conflicting – histories. Understanding and valuing this complexity is core to understanding community.

Compassion

Compassion is an important attribute of a healthy community. When a community includes several ways to serve its members, through social service organizations and community-building organizations, and in other ways, it demonstrates compassion for community members. As noted earlier, this book uses an asset-based model, and compassion is an asset that is often undervalued. Peter Block notes,

> We marginalize compassion in the public conversation. . . . Having a large number of social services in a neighborhood is seen as a weakness, not a selling point. The view is that if people need help, if they are vulnerable or in crisis, it is a communal liability. The generosity that serves these people goes unmentioned as an asset.
>
> *2008, p. 44*

And as the International Campaign for Compassionate Communities notes,

> A community where compassion is fully alive is a thriving, resilient community whose members are moved by empathy to take compassionate action, are able to confront crises with innovative solutions, are confident in navigating changes in the economy and the environment, and are resilient enough to bounce back readily from natural and man-made disasters. . . . A compassionate community is one where *people are motivated by compassion to take responsibility for and care for each other.*
>
> *Charter for Compassion International, 2016*

Social Capital: Core Elements

Social capital was defined earlier in this chapter, and this section delves deeper into its core elements. The Saguaro Seminar, based at Harvard University and reflecting Robert Putnam's work (see Chapter 3), conducts research about communities. Its *Social Capital Community Benchmark Survey: Executive Summary* includes comprehensive descriptions of the core elements of social capital that it has identified. These definitions are applicable for this discussion about the characteristics of community and have been included in their entirety:

Trust

Social trust: at the core of social capital is the question of whether you can trust other people. Often this trust is forged with specific people through common participation in groups, associations, and activities. Nevertheless, when this trust transcends from trust of *specific* individuals to generalized trust, it is extraordinarily valuable. Our first index of social trust combines trust of people in one's neighborhood, coworkers, shop clerks, co-religionists, local police, and finally "most people."

Inter-racial trust: a critical challenge facing communities attempting to build social capital is the fact that it is simply harder to do in places that are more diverse. The measure of inter-racial trust looks at the extent to which different racial groups (whites, blacks, Hispanics, and Asians) trust one another and is thus one proxy for the health of inter-racial relations in a community.

Diversity of friendships

Equally important to their levels of social trust are how diverse people's social networks are. This index broadly measures the degree to which people's social networks (and collectively a community's networks) are diverse. These "bridging ties" are especially valuable in producing community solidarity and in forging a larger consensus on how communities need to change or work together.

Political participation

Conventional politics participation: One of the key measures for how engaged we are in communities is the extent to which we are involved politically. This measure looks at how many in our communities are registered to vote, actually vote, express interest in politics, are knowledgeable about political affairs and read the newspaper regularly.

Protest politics participation: The data in the Social Capital Community Benchmark Survey indicate that many communities that exhibit low levels of participation in conventional/electoral ways, nonetheless exhibit high levels of participation in protest forms, such as taking part in marches, demonstrations, boycotts, rallies, participating in groups that took action for local reform, participating in labor and ethnically-related groups. This dimension is a composite of those types of participation.

Civic leadership and associational involvement

Many people typically get involved locally by joining groups that they care about (be they veterans groups, sports groups, literary groups, or new age poetry clubs). We measured such engagement in two ways:

Civic Leadership: this is a composite measure both of how frequently respondents were engaged in groups, clubs and local discussions of town or school affairs, and also whether the respondent took a leadership role within these groups. Communities that rank high on this aspect of social capital benefit from a hum of civic activity.

Associational involvement: we measured associational involvement across 18 broad categories of groups (including an "other" category). Respondents were asked about participation in the following types of groups: organizations affiliated with religion; sports clubs, leagues, or outdoor activities; youth organizations; parent associations or other school support groups; veterans groups; neighborhood associations; seniors groups; charity or social welfare organizations; labor unions; professional, trade, farm or business associations; service or fraternal organizations; ethnic, nationality, or civil rights organizations; political groups; literary, art, or musical groups; hobby, investment, or garden clubs; self-help programs; groups that meet only over the Internet; and any other type of groups or associations.

Informal socializing

While many communities (or individuals) are either higher or lower generally in social capital, some communities or individuals are more likely to develop social connections through formal memberships and associations ("machers") and others are more likely to develop these connections through informal friendships ("schmoozers"). While the "civic leadership" and "associational involvement" measures above capture the formal social ties, the "informal socializing" dimension measures the degree to which residents had friends over to their home, hung out with friends in a public place, socialized with co-workers outside of work, played cards or board games with others, and visited with relatives.

Giving and volunteering

One of the ways that Americans express their concern for others is through giving to charity or volunteering. Various aspects of generosity go together: people who are generous with their purse are also generous with their time. The same is true of communities. This dimension measures how often community residents volunteer at various venues and how generous they are in giving.

Faith-based engagement

Religion in America is a big part of social capital. Roughly one-half of all American connectedness is religious or religiously affiliated, whether measured by memberships, volunteering time, or philanthropy. Thus, this dimension matters a lot to overall levels of community connection. This measure of faith-based engagement looks at: religious attendance and membership, participation in church activities besides services, participation in organization affiliated with religion, giving to religious causes and volunteering at place of worship.

Equality of civic engagement across the community

In some communities the ranks of the civic are much more heavily skewed towards those who are wealthier, more educated, and whiter. In other communities, the poor, less educated, and people of color participate at rates much closer to their wealthier, whiter and more educated brethren. Since it is important to the community health, this measure scores highly those communities with more egalitarian civic participation. [This measure is an average correlation across eight different types of civic participation and across three measures of class (race, income, and education) to see how skewed civic participation in a community is.] (The Saguaro Seminar, 2000, pp. 8–10)

This excellent list is useful in examining one's own work and the work of others, including the examples used in this book. In each case, consider this: Do these organizations work better because they have more of these elements?

Keep these terms in mind throughout, noting your evolving understanding of what the terms mean. You will gain a deeper understanding of the rich and complex ways that these terms are used. They are included because they are relevant to the ways that museums and cultural organizations can be vital members of their communities. The relationships one develops and nurtures are social capital, and the *degree* of relationship – how strong or deep it is – is also social capital.

Core Values That Support Community Involvement

This section addresses the core values that form the bedrock of museum–community involvement. Cultivating these values will support museum staff and leadership in all their endeavors and are at the heart of community involvement.

Respect is a core value and a key component of community, to be embraced and practiced with one's communities and internally within one's organization. What does respect look like in practice? Pay attention to how other community members act, and follow their lead. Often, this will mean listening, not interrupting, and responding/following up on what people say. It may mean stepping aside so that others may lead. It will mean thanking people, providing the space so others can go first if they would like, providing refreshments, and other considerate actions. Different people may have different ideas of what respectful behavior looks like, so it is a good idea to pay attention and ask first.

Empathy, the ability to understand the feelings of another, is a core value embedded in the life and work of community involvement. Being able to understand others takes one out of one's own limited perspective. It challenges one's biases and preconceived notions.

True listening is a skill, and it is a core value of community involvement. When one truly listens, one focuses on what a person is saying. As Tibetan Buddhist leader Sakyong Mipham Rinpoche (2015) notes in his True Listening blog, "[B]y learning to listen, we can digest, contemplate, and engage in the thoughts of another, understanding and responding to their emotional state." Rinpoche further notes, "When we are unable to listen, we lose connectivity." *Connectivity* is a core aspect of all our relationships and the basis of our work.

Bibliography

American Alliance of Museums. (n.d.). Assessment types: Community engagement assessment. Retrieved from http://www.aam-us.org/resources/assessment-programs/MAP/assessment-types

American Association of Museums (Ed.). (2002). *Mastering civic engagement: A challenge to museums*. Washington, DC: American Association of Museums.

Animating Democracy. (n.d.a). *What is social change? Terms of arts, culture, and cultural change*. Retrieved from http://www.animatingdemocracy.org/place-start/what-social-change#community-engagement

Animating Democracy. (n.d.b). *What is social change? Terms of social change*. Retrieved from http://www.animatingdemocracy.org/place-start/what-social-change#civic-engagement

Beavers, K. A., & Hodgson, K. (2011). *Arts and culture briefing paper 04: How arts and cultural strategies enhance community engagement and participation*. Washington, DC: American Planning Association. Retrieved from https://www.planning.org/research/arts/briefingpapers/engagement.htm

Block, P. (2008). *Community: The structure of belonging*. San Francisco: Berrett-Koehler.

Canadian Career Development Foundation. (n.d.). *Working with community stakeholders: Developing relationships*. Ottawa, Ontario: Canadian Career Development Foundation. Retrieved from http://www.ccdf.ca/ccdf/NewCoach/english/ccoacha/issue_a1b_developing.htm

Charter for Compassion International. (2016). International Campaign for Compassionate Communities. Bainbridge Island, WA. Retrieved from http://www.charterforcompassion.org/communities

The Harwood Group. (1999). *Community rhythms: Five stages of community life*. Flint, MI: The Harwood Institute. Retrieved from https://static1.squarespace.com/static/5602cde4e4b04430b90a97fd/t/56afa385b09f95bf0e12088e/1454351239542/CommunityRhythmsReport.pdf?utm_source=Enews+9%2F29%2F16&utm_campaign=enews+9%2F29%2F16&utm_medium=email

Kretzmann, J. P., & McKnight, J. L. (1993). *Building communities from the inside out: A path toward finding and mobilizing a community's assets*. Chicago: ACTA Publications.

Museums Association (2016). *Valuing diversity: The case for inclusive museums*. Retrieved from http://www.museumsassociation.org/download?id=1194934

O'Mara, J., & Richter, A. (2016). *Global diversity & inclusion benchmarks: Standards for organizations around the world*. Washington, DC: The Diversity Collegium. Retrieved from http://www.diversitycollegium.org/usertools/GDIB-V-03072016-3-2MB.pdf

Putnam, R. (2000). *Bowling alone*. New York: Simon & Schuster.

Rinpoche, Sakyong Mipham. (2015, March 16). True Listening blog. Retrieved from http://shambhalatimes.org/2015/03/16/true-listening-2/

Saegert, S. (2006). *Community building and civic capacity*. New York: CUNY Graduate Center and Aspen Institute Roundtable on Community Change. Retrieved from https://assets.aspeninstitute.org/content/uploads/files/content/docs/rcc/CommunityBuildingCivicCapacity.pdf

The Saguaro Seminar. (2000). *Social capital community benchmark survey: Executive summary*. Cambridge, MA: Harvard Kennedy School. Retrieved from https://www.hks.harvard.edu/saguaro/communitysurvey/docs/exec_summ.pdf

Smith, M. K. (n.d.). What is community? The encyclopedia of informal education. Retrieved from http://www.infed.org/community/community.htm

2

BUILDING HEALTHIER COMMUNITIES

The research included here about building healthier communities helps museum professionals learn about their communities and guide their museums on the journey to community involvement. The approaches in this chapter – community well-being, collective impact, and community anchors/community catalysts – are comprehensive approaches, bringing together people and organizations from multiple sectors to accomplish the goal of building healthier communities.

Community Well-Being

Much of museum–community involvement work is based on the idea of museums as vital members of their communities, integral to building healthier communities and contributing to a community's well-being. Community well-being is a term applied in public health, community development, and social science research, among others. The University of Minnesota's Center for Spirituality & Healing description is relevant for cultural organizations' understanding of community well-being:

> Community wellbeing is the combination of social, economic, environmental, cultural, and political conditions identified by individuals and their communities as essential for them to flourish and fulfill their potential.
>
> When we look at community as a whole, we find three attributes that play a large role in wellbeing: connectedness, livability, and equity. We can explore each of these attributes to find factors that contribute to community wellbeing.

Connectedness

Connection is fostered by a community's social networks that:

- Offer social support
- Enhance social trust

- Support members living harmoniously together
- Foster civic engagement
- Empower members to participate in community and democracy

Livability

A livable community is supported by the infrastructure, including:

- Housing
- Transportation
- Education
- Parks and recreation
- Human services
- Public safety
- Access to culture and the arts

Equity

An equitable community is supported by values of diversity, social justice, and individual empowerment, where:

- All members are treated with fairness and justice
- Basic needs are met (adequate access to health services, decent housing, food, personal security)
- There is equal opportunity to get education and meet individual potential
  University of Minnesota's Center for Spirituality & Healing, 2013.

A close review of these attributes reveals a number of connections and ways that museums and cultural organizations can be vital contributors to community well-being. All the attributes are characterized by a sense of *sufficiency*. A healthy community has sufficient resources so that every person feels safe and has access to the resources to live a healthy life: healthy food that is reasonably priced, shelter, schools, community gathering places, businesses, and areas for outdoor activities, including well-maintained parks.

Creating and supporting healthy communities (community well-being) is a focus for several sectors. The field of human development provides an approach that is relevant for museums and cultural organizations, as it includes many aspects of human and community health, such as engagement in community life and environmental sustainability. A well-known effort in supporting healthy communities is the Human Development Index (HDI), developed in 1990 by the United Nations Development Programme (UNDP). In a post on the Createquity blog in August 2015, writers Talia Gibas, Ian David Moss, John Carnwath, Katie Ingersoll, and Fari Nzinga described the HDI:

> The HDI is relatively simple. Its three dimensions are "a long and healthy life," "being knowledgeable," and a "decent standard of living." The indicators

are life expectancy at birth, mean years of schooling for adults over 25 and expected years of schooling for young children (calculated via a mix of UNESCO statistics and actual enrollment figures), and gross national income per capita. The geometric mean of numerical scores from these four indicators comprise the final HDI index score for any particular country.

2015, August 31.

Gibas and colleagues go on to describe other well-being measures as:

- relationships with family and friends
- emotional well-being
- material well-being
- health
- work and productive activity
- feeling a part of one's local community
- personal safety.

By considering each of these qualities separately, museum leadership and staff can create a set of measures to guide the community-based work of cultural organizations and museums. For instance, to what degree do the museum's exhibitions inspire and provide a place for people to deepen their relationships with family and friends? Are there mechanisms in place to stimulate thoughtful conversations and dialogue? Are there safe spaces for nurturing the emotional well-being of people within the museum and in the community? A museum may have incorporated these spaces for dialogue and reflection within an exhibition because they are accepted professional practice. When they also recognize that these spaces serve a purpose of promoting well-being, museum leadership and staff begin to see their work in new ways. See Chapter 8 for additional questions to help guide this process.

Another example is the American Human Development Project, which uses various measures to indicate well-being in communities. Their *Measure of America* series asks pertinent questions and provides descriptions of communities in California:

What will California look like decades from now? Will life in 2040 be better or worse, and for whom? One way to answer these critical questions is to explore how today's children—tomorrow's adults—are faring.

Measure of America's *A Portrait of California 2014–2015* does just that. The report uses health, education, and income indicators to sort communities across the state into five distinct "Californias" defined not by geography but by well-being and access to opportunity. And it shows how growing inequality is increasingly setting our kids on very different life paths.

Burd-Sharps and Lewis, 2014, p. 4

The report goes on to say,

Instead of relying on traditional economic analysis, Measure of America's *A Portrait of California* uses the human development approach to tell us how people are doing. Three dimensions—a long and healthy life, access to knowledge, and a decent standard of living—are examined in detail and presented along a simple ten-point scale: the American Human Development (HD) Index.

Burd-Sharps and Lewis, 2014, p. 7

The human development approach is useful as a framework within which to see the work of museums in building healthier communities and promoting community well-being.

Collective Impact

Collective impact is a theory of social change focused on cross-sector collaboration to address complex social problems. Collective impact, a term initially developed by Mark Kramer and John Kania at FSG consulting firm, encompasses core ways to collaborate to effect community change. Through studying many social change efforts worldwide, Kramer, Kania, and their colleagues identified five conditions for success, and they became the five core elements of collective impact. They are:

- Establishing a common goal (sometimes called a common agenda): The participants in the collective impact initiative collectively create a shared vision and a common understanding of the core issues, including developing a common language to describe the issues. This alignment, mutual understanding, and agreement on what terminology to use and what it means are at the core of effective collaborative work, and establishing a common goal is very helpful in illuminating assumptions and clarifying expectations.
- Tracking progress using the same measures: The individual organizations participating collect the same types of data and measure results using the same yardstick and consistent methods of reporting. This provides a way to look at comparable data, ensuring that the information from the various organizations is in alignment, and it helps keep everyone on track.
- Each participating organization focuses on the work that it does best, and in this way the organizations mutually reinforce one another. It is the coordination of these various activities that leverages the entire collective's work.
- Communicating frequently and consistently: Consistent communication facilitates the work tremendously, and in-person communications are very effective in building the interpersonal relationships and trust that make collective impact initiatives most effective.
- Having a set of skilled and dedicated resources to support the collective, ongoing efforts. This is often provided by a separate organization – a backbone organization – whose resources are fully dedicated to the initiative and solely focused on the initiative. This allows the

participants, who also have their own work (or agenda) to adhere to, to focus on that work.

University of Kansas Work Group for Community
Health and Development Community Tool Box, n.d.

Collective impact has direct relevance for museums and cultural organizations as they strive to work more closely with their communities to address complex social problems. Collective impact is defined and used in different ways, and it is appropriate for some, but not all situations. When an issue is not complex, other approaches may be very effective. Collective impact is a comprehensive approach, and small organizations may feel that it is beyond their capacity to learn about and incorporate it completely into their practice. If they were to consider each primary aspect of collective impact and determine a few practices that they could easily incorporate to get them started, it would help them look at what they do with fresh eyes.

With these components of a healthy community in mind, museum leaders and staff can now consider the vital role of museums and cultural organizations. Cultural organizations have assets: people (staff, board members, volunteers, members, colleagues, etc.), connections (social capital), space (real estate, such as buildings, rooms, outdoor spaces, parking lots, and classrooms), exhibitions, programs, collections, knowledge, and financial resources. These are all part of the resources that the museum can bring to the work of building healthier communities.

Building Community

The term *building community* is used to describe a variety of situations and desires, from deepening the relationships with teams to developing resources and skills within one's groups and neighborhoods. There is even the popular "How to Build Community" poster, created by Karen Kerney of Syracuse Cultural Workers, which includes tips such as "Know your neighbors," "Use your library," "Listen to elders," and "Share your skills." In considering this term, consider what building community looks like. Does it mean a community where the person-to-person and group-to-group connections are growing stronger? What are the elements that are important in building community? What are the indicators that describe a community that is becoming more vibrant?

The Aspen Institute Roundtable on Community Change describes building community as democratic or participatory efforts to enhance the capacities of individuals and organizations in communities and the connections between them, and the efforts to engage and represent the community as a whole. Patricia Auspos, Aspen senior fellow, says,

[C]ommunity building is an important precursor to community change because it builds a platform that can be instrumental in accomplishing other things. This is typically done by engaging residents in a process that involves analysis of a problem, assessment of community strengths and weaknesses, exploration of possible solutions, articulation of what the community wants or does not want, and development of an agenda for change. This process builds trust and networks, mobilizes the community for action, gives legitimacy to plans, and lays the groundwork for future change.

[I]n addition to creating a platform for action, community building contributes to improved programmatic outcomes by developing the following types of capacities among residents and organizations within the community:

- The capacity to galvanize and support changes in individual behavior, including getting residents to work together on common problems. This is particularly important when the outcomes sought are sensitive to changes in personal behavior and measured at the individual level – e.g., health outcomes and employment outcomes.
- The capacity to manage, operate and implement programs and services, and the capacity to manage multi-organizational partnerships and multi-component projects. These capacities are particularly important when the outside systems and institutions are not functioning adequately, and community organizations or groups decide to take on critical functions themselves.
- The capacity to affect outside actors and win changes in policy or practice that benefit the community and its residents. . . . It allows communities to influence external conditions and decisions that can influence how residents behave and the opportunities that are available to them.

Auspos, 2005, pp. 4,5

The term is also used more casually to describe creating more extensive and deeper connections with individuals and organizations in one's own communities.

Social Well-Being

Social well-being is a way to think about what a healthy community entails. It includes many aspects, such as housing quality, school effectiveness, economic and ethnic diversity, political engagement, environmental health, security (physical and social), economic well-being and vitality, physical and mental health, and social connection (including the presence and involvement of cultural resources). Assessing communities through these lenses shows the degree of community health and well-being, and it shows how museums and libraries can contribute to community well-being through their programs and activities.

Using these two frameworks – collective impact and social well-being – provides a set of tools for approaching long-term community change. They provide mechanisms and processes for initiating and sustaining partnerships, measuring the short-term and long-term impacts of community-focused initiatives, and new ways to engage more deeply with community members. They can also provide a framework to assess overall museum activities. As museum staff reviews programs and assesses them according to various criteria (e.g., to what degree does this program align with our mission? To what degree does it serve our priority audiences?), it is possible to add new questions relating to social and community well-being (e.g., to what degree does this program serve to improve the quality of the local environment? To what degree does this program increase social connection and the level of trust in the community?). For a museum deeply committed to community involvement, using the lenses of social well-being and collective impact to look at their programs will show what they are doing and what impact they are having.

Community Anchors and Community Catalysts

The Institute of Museum and Library Services (IMLS) includes community anchors in its funding criteria in the Museums for America and National Leadership grant programs. According to the IMLS, "IMLS promotes the role of museums as essential partners in addressing the needs of their communities by leveraging their expertise, knowledge, physical space, technology, and other resources to identify and implement solutions" (n.d.).

A community anchor is an institution that is an active part of neighborhood revitalization. It is often a big employer, like a university or hospital, one that can have a major impact in the community. Museums and libraries can fill these roles as community-centered organizations with a social mission. Their community revitalization work can focus on the physical revitalization, such as when they are building a new facility or animating public spaces; they can focus on community building, serving as safe places where community members come together, and as places for bringing together partners for collective impact, providing a place for comprehensive economic, educational, and social services to benefit communities.

The IMLS Community Catalyst initiative, begun in 2016, is intricately linked to community well-being, with the intent to help museums and libraries understand their role as contributors to community vitality. The Community Catalyst initiative focuses on how museums and libraries seek to address community challenges and spark change. In the report *Strengthening Networks, Sparking Change: Museums and Libraries as Community Catalysts*, published by IMLS in January 2017, authors Michael H. Norton and Emily Dowdall note that museums and libraries are taking this call to action seriously, and many are striving to serve as catalysts for positive change in their communities. They note that the collective impact and social well-being conceptual frameworks are very useful for museums and libraries considering deeper community involvement. Museums and libraries can learn how anchor institutions are shifting and expanding their roles in their local communities. They are not only focusing on their core work in their core locations but are also doing core work in new locations and expanding their services beyond their core missions.

Research and Publications

The premise of this book advocates for museums and cultural organizations to be much more actively involved with building healthier communities. This means learning about one's communities, and there is a great deal of current research that is relevant and very useful. Funders, especially foundations and the Institute of Museum and Library Services, are often the instigators of this research. The information they provide helps museum leadership and staff understand more about their communities. This commitment to addressing inequality and supporting equity in communities means that museums and cultural organizations have an opportunity to learn from social change efforts in specific programs and to see how their work aligns with these community change efforts.

Several foundations noted below are publishing material relevant for museums and cultural organizations involving their communities. Their focus may be communities, inclusion, or cultural organizations. This is a sampling; there are several foundations whose work is vital to their communities that were not included in these pages, and the reader is encouraged to seek additional information.

The information and publications from foundations that focus on inclusion are relevant in the work of museums being involved with their communities. When inclusion is intentional, involvement happens more readily. Each of the foundations noted below shares information about inclusion and supporting community health and well-being.

Foundations and other agencies have the resources to guide museum leadership and staff as they embark on learning about communities. Their reports are usually freely available on their websites (see the bibliography at the end of this chapter to link to a number of reports). Foundations work with knowledgeable researchers who ask relevant questions and can provide meaningful information. The researchers have already posed many of the questions museums might pose themselves; reading reports in the early stages of community work will inform the leadership and staff about relevant concerns early. These reports provide the backbone of information that is very useful for learning about communities. These reports often include lessons and tips that are useful guidelines for museums and cultural organizations as they engage in community involvement. They illuminate current projects and challenges that colleagues are encountering and provide new perspectives in addressing these challenges.

W. K. Kellogg Foundation

In January 2016, the W. K. Kellogg Foundation announced that it was advancing its Truth, Racial Healing & Transformation (TRHT) initiative, working with a diverse group of organizations. As WKKF (2016) notes,

> Specifically, the TRHT enterprise will prioritize inclusive, community-based healing activities and policy design that seek to change collective community

narratives and broaden the understanding that Americans have for their diverse experiences.

Museums and cultural organizations, with their capacity to showcase the changed collective community narratives, have a role to play and should be at the table in initiatives such as these. As Ramón Murguía, WKKF board chair, notes, "There are thousands of untold stories in communities of color that must be shared to shape authentic perceptions of our lives" (W. K. Kellogg Foundation, 2016).

In addition, the Kellogg Foundation (n.d.a) notes,

> We believe that people have the inherent capacity to solve their own problems and that social transformation is within the reach of all communities. We act on this belief by partnering with diverse communities, amplifying their voices and helping them to create conditions in which their children can thrive.

The James Irvine Foundation

The James Irvine Foundation has been delving deeply into engagement in the arts and asking (and being asked) challenging questions. In a series of posts in January 2016, the foundation asked, "Are we doing enough?" (Russell and Garcés, 2016; Russell, Helstrup-Alvarez, Allen, Evans, and Novick, 2016). It looked at what recipients of the Irvine's New California Arts Fund grants have learned since the New California Arts Fund launched in 2014. As Ted Russell, Irvine's senior program officer for the arts, notes, "In the two years since, this initial group of arts organizations has tried and explored and succeeded and failed and learned about the many tools and practices they need to become more resilient organizations, to better reflect California's changing population, and to uphold their value to their community."

The Irvine Foundation has published several useful reports and tools. The Exploring Engagement Fund is part of the foundation's arts program, and the lessons and tools are useful for many types of organizations. The *Emerging Lessons and Implications from the Exploring Engagement Fund* publication in October 2014 includes a lesson about partnering:

Lesson#3 Partner well
Community partners are critical to accessing new and diverse participants.
    Grantees cited community partners as one of the most important factors in the success — and one of the greatest lasting benefits — of their projects. They engaged a variety of partners, from the expected such as social service organizations, community centers, government agencies, educational institutions, libraries and churches, to the unexpected such as a skate shop, a bar, local farms and an anarchist sewing collective.
    Most grantees did not start their engagement work with these relationships fully developed. They had to learn that their own interest in reaching

low-income groups and communities of color was not sufficient to ensure the participation of needed partners. Yet the involvement of these partners was essential to the hard work of building credibility with new participants.

It takes time to find partners who can be relied on to open doors, and to build trust with these partners. Arts organizations must demonstrate that they respect the work and role of each partner. In building these relationships, many arts organizations learned to relinquish some control of the participant experience to partners in exchange for the increased access that partnerships provide.

Most grantees want to continue their partner relationships. Community partners have provided input and guidance on project design, access to target participants, marketing support and facilities. They have helped grantees gain credibility and a deeper reach into communities.

Practical Tip: Work with well-regarded, active local organizations

Join with community partners that are knowledgeable about, and connected to, the population you seek to engage. Don't start with a fixed, preconceived plan; assume your partners' needs and interests are as important to the project as your own. Establish common commitment, shared expectations, goals and values, then create a written agreement (e.g., a Memorandum of Understanding). Build in time to develop the relationship. Assume you will have less control than usual. Be adaptable in the process; expect unanticipated changes and challenges based on your partners' organizational dynamics, capacity issues or lack of familiarity with arts organizations or the arts in general.

Excerpted from Emerging Lessons and Implications from the Exploring Engagement Fund, *a Harder+Company Community Research report on the first phase of the James Irvine Foundation's Exploring Engagement Fund, October 2014*

Nathan Cummings Foundation

The Nathan Cummings Foundation is supporting Americans for the Arts' Animating Democracy EQUITY 360 project. EQUITY 360 is an online resource designed to inform and guide grant makers who seek to establish more equitable funding programs and practices. As the Animating Democracy program notes,

Arts funding and policy cannot perpetuate inequity and discrimination while at the same time promoting the arts as bridge builders and agents for equity in communities. To achieve cultural equity (fair and equitable access to cultural resources and support) as well as equity through arts and culture will require redesign or creation of funding programs, relevant eligibility and review criteria, and improved communications to reach new applicants, in addition to changes in evaluation practices.

Animating Democracy, n.d.

The Ford Foundation

The Ford Foundation is engaged in research about global trends, and this research has led to a commitment to address inequality and support equity in communities. As Darren Walker, president of the Ford Foundation wrote in the foundation's Equals Change blog on June 11, 2015 (excerpted here):

> Broadly stated, we found five factors that consistently contribute to inequality:
>
> - Cultural narratives that undermine fairness, tolerance and inclusion
> - Unequal access to government decision-making and resources
> - Persistent prejudice and discrimination against women as well as racial, ethnic and caste minorities
> - Rules of the economy that magnify unequal opportunity and outcomes
> - The failure to invest in and protect vital public goods, such as education and natural resources
>
> **Where we're going**
>
> To address and respond to these drivers of inequality, we will be working in six program areas, very much reflective of the five drivers. They are:
>
> - Civic Engagement and Government
> - Creativity and Free Expression
> - Gender, Ethnic, and Racial Justice
> - Inclusive Economies
> - Internet Freedom
> - Youth Opportunity and Learning
>
> These six thematic areas will not be silos, each unto itself. They are ingredients that each of our offices—depending on local context and the priorities set by local partners—will combine in creative ways to disrupt the drivers of inequality. We suspect that in many cases the most dynamic frontlines of social change will be found not within these six areas, but at the intersections where they connect. And our commitment to human rights and human dignity will be at the center of all of them.

Weingart Foundation

The Weingart Foundation is committed to equity. A few excerpts from the message from the chairman and the president (Monica C. Lozano, chairman of the board, and Fred Ali, president and CEO) posted on the foundation's website on August 16, 2016, include the following:

We are also hearing from grantees that lasting change will require a collective and long-term focus that addresses the underlying circumstances that create and perpetuate inequity, the root of so many of our most intractable problems.

This is why the Weingart Foundation is making a full commitment to equity—a long-term commitment to base all of our policy and program decisions on achieving the goal to advance fairness, inclusion, and opportunity for all Southern Californians—especially those communities hit hardest by persistent poverty.

We recognize that inequity stems from the historic, long-term barriers to rights and opportunities endured by low-income communities, including those Southern Californians whose skin color, ethnicity, gender, immigration status, disability, age, sexual orientation, or zip code has prevented them from realizing the dignities and liberties all people deserve. We have a responsibility to invest in the communities that have been excluded and under-resourced, so they can realize their full potential. It's a matter of justice.

To advance equity requires an examination of privilege, including the power dynamics between funders and nonprofits. Our full commitment to equity will also require the Foundation to constantly examine our own internal policies, practices, and culture with regard to equity and inclusion.

This is complex work, and the Weingart Foundation does not have all the answers. Nor are these issues going to be solved overnight. But we have a plan for how to begin and are committed to learning from, and partnering with, nonprofits and the people who experience inequity first-hand. We are also committed to challenging ourselves to work with a sense of urgency and to take risks.

Lozano and Ali, 2016

The Andrew W. Mellon Foundation

The Andrew W. Mellon Foundation supports research and initiatives focusing on inclusion and diversity. Its publication *Our Compelling Interests: The Value of Diversity for Democracy and a Prosperous Society* (2016) investigates how diversity and social connectedness are imperative to communities' shared success. The Mellon Foundation partnered with the Association of Art Museum Directors and the American Alliance of Museums to conduct a demographic survey and published the *Art Museum Staff Demographic Survey* (Schonfeld, Westermann, and Sweeney, 2015), spurring numerous conversations and commentary. The foundation continues to support this work. In February 2017, building on the *Art Museum Staff Demographic Survey* study, the Mellon Foundation announced it would support a set of case studies "designed to guide museum leadership teams in creating successful, forward-thinking plans to improve diversity and inclusivity in their staffing practices" (Andrew W. Mellon Foundation, 2017).

The Wallace Foundation

The Wallace Foundation has long supported community work and the arts. Its research and publications focused on building arts audiences include *The Road to Results: Effective Practices for Building Arts Audiences*, written by Bob Harlow in 2014. Its earlier publications include *Opening the Door to the Entire Community: How Museums Are Using Permanent Collections to Engage Audiences* (Lila Wallace-Reader's Digest Fund, 1998) and *Engaging the Entire Community: A New Role for Permanent Collections* (Lila Wallace-Reader's Digest Fund, 1999). The Wallace Foundation is keenly aware of the importance of sharing information, noting, "Our approach to accomplishing our mission emerges from the idea that foundations have a unique but often untapped capacity to develop evidence and experiences that can help advance an entire field" (The Wallace Foundation, n.d.).

Partners for Livable Communities

Partners for Livable Communities is a nonprofit organization focused on restoring and renewing communities. Its mission is "To improve the quality of life and economic and social wellbeing of low- and moderate-income individuals and communities" (n.d.). Its publications include *Culture Connects All: Rethinking Audiences in Times of Demographic Change* in 2011 and *Stories for Change* in 2012.

The International Coalition of Sites of Conscience

The International Coalition of Sites of Conscience is a membership organization that provides support for its members to deeply engage in community building. As the coalition notes on its website, "We build the capacity of Sites of Conscience to develop, share and adapt innovative public programs that move people from memory to action." The coalition is a "global network of historic sites, museums, and memory initiatives connecting past struggles to today's movements for human rights and social justice." Understanding that building capacity and mutual support for engaging in this is crucial to effective work, the coalition provides its members, as well as nonmembers, with training in early community engagement work connecting the past to the present, evaluating the impact, and leading the change through strategic planning. Coalition members are eligible to apply for project support (up to $10,000) for capacity-building projects, participate in trainings and conferences, utilize the online resource center, and connect with one another in mutual support (International Coalition of Sites of Conscience, n.d.).

Bibliography

Animating Democracy, Americans for the Arts. (n.d.). EQUITY 360: Grantmaking. Retrieved from http://animatingdemocracy.org/equity-360-grantmaking

Andrew W. Mellon Foundation. (2016, August 15). Our compelling interests: The value of diversity for democracy and a prosperous society. [Press release]. Retrieved from https://mellon.org/resources/news/articles/our-compelling-interests-diversity/

Andrew W. Mellon Foundation. (2017, February 22). Mellon Foundation to fund a series of case studies on diversity to guide art museum leadership on future inclusivity efforts. [Press release]. Retrieved from https://mellon.org/resources/news/articles/mellon-foundation-fund-series-case-studies-diversity-guide-art-museum-leadership-future-inclusivity-efforts/

Auspos, P. (2005). The contribution of community building project: Crosscutting issues and lessons. New York, NY: Aspen Institute Roundtable on Community Change. Retrieved from https://assets.aspeninstitute.org/content/uploads/files/content/upload/rccfinalcrosscuttingreport.pdf

Bergeron, A., & Tuttle, B. (2013). *Magnetic: The art and science of engagement.* Washington, DC: AAM Press.

Burd-Sharps, S., & Lewis, K. (2014). *A portrait of California 2014–2015.* New York: American Human Development Project. Foreword, p. 4, Key Findings, p. 7. Retrieved from http://ssrc-static.s3.amazonaws.com/wp-content/uploads/2014/12/A-Portrait-of-California_vF.pdf

Chinn, C., Reddy, P., Sajadian, M., & Shwartzman, S. (2015, April). *Will you miss me when I'm gone? Positioning your museum as a core community resource.* Session conducted at the annual meeting of the American Alliance of Museums, Atlanta, GA.

Dilenschneider, C. (2015, November 11). Data reveals the best thing about visiting a cultural organization [Blog post]. Retrieved from http://colleendilen.com/2015/11/11/data-reveals-the-best-thing-about-visiting-a-cultural-organization-fast-fact-video/

FSG Reimagining Social Change. (n.d.). Collective impact. Retrieved from http://www.fsg.org/ideas-in-action/collective-impact

Gibas, T., Moss, I. D., Carnwath, J., Ingersoll, K., & Nzinga, F. (2015, August 31). Part of your world: On the arts and wellbeing [Blog post; refers to United Nations Development Programme (UDNP) at http://hdr.undp.org/en/content/human-development-index-hdi]. Retrieved from http://createquity.com/2015/08/part-of-your-world-on-the-arts-and-wellbeing/?utm_source=Createquity&utm_campaign=809b5fc8dd-Createquity+email+blast&utm_medium=email&utm_term=0_05d97ced75-809b5fc8dd-291090073

Harlow, B. (2014). *The road to results: Effective practices for building arts audiences.* New York: The Wallace Foundation. Retrieved from http://www.wallacefoundation.org/knowledge-center/Documents/The-Road-to-Results-Effective-Practices-for-Building-Arts-Audiences.pdf

Institute of Museum and Library Services. (n.d.). Museums for America. Retrieved from https://www.imls.gov/grants/available/museums-america

International Coalition of Sites of Conscience. (n.d.). Approach. Retrieved from http://www.sitesofconscience.org/approach/

Kerney, K. (1998). Poster: How to build community. Syracuse, NY: Syracuse Cultural Workers. Retrieved from https://www.syracuseculturalworkers.com/products/poster-how-to-build-community

Lewis, E. (2016, May). *Diversity: From talk to action.* Session conducted at the annual meeting of the American Alliance of Museums, Washington, DC.

Libraries Transforming Communities. (n.d.). Chicago, IL: American Library Association. Retrieved from http://www.ala.org/transforminglibraries/libraries-transforming-communities

Lila Wallace-Reader's Digest Fund. (1998). *Opening the door to the entire community: How museums are using permanent collections to engage audiences.* New York: Lila Wallace-Reader's Digest Fund. Retrieved from http://www.wallacefoundation.org/knowledge-center/Documents/Permanent-Collections-to-Engage-Audiences.pdf

Lila Wallace-Reader's Digest Fund. (1999). *Engaging the entire community: A new role for permanent collections.* New York: Lila Wallace-Reader's Digest Fund. Retrieved from http://www.wallacefoundation.org/knowledge-center/Documents/New-Role-for-Permanent-Collections.pdf

Local Initiatives Support Corporation and Institute of Museum and Library Services. (2015, November 11). *Museums, libraries and comprehensive initiatives: A first look at emerging experience.* Retrieved from http://www.instituteccd.org/uploads/iccd/documents/final_museum_and_library_report_layout.pdf

Lozano, M., & Ali, F. (2016, August). Weingart Foundation message from the chairman and the president: A full commitment to equity. Retrieved from http://www.weingartfnd.org/August-2016-Presidents-Message

Norton, M., & Dowdall, E. (2017, January). *Strengthening networks, sparking change: Museums and libraries as community catalysts 2016.* Washington, DC: Institute of Museum and Library Services. Retrieved from https://www.imls.gov/sites/default/files/publications/documents/community-catalyst-report-january-2017.pdf

Partners for Livable Communities. (2011). *Culture connects all: Rethinking audiences in times of demographic change.* Retrieved from http://livable.org/livability-resources/reports-a-publications/520-culture-connects-all-

Partners for Livable Communities. (2012). *Stories for change.* Retrieved from http://livable.org/livability-resources/reports-a-publications/564-stories-for-change-

Partners for Livable Communities. (n.d.). Mission & methodology. Retrieved from http://www.livable.org/about-us/mission-a-history

Putnam, R. (2000). *Bowling alone.* New York: Simon & Schuster.

Russell, T., & Garcés, M. (2016, January 19). Are we doing enough? Part 1: Tough questions we get asked about engagement practices and programming in the arts. [Blog post]. Read the full series at www.irvine.org/arts. Retrieved from https://medium.com/new-faces-new-spaces/are-we-doing-enough-part-1-58215ffa3824#.fw0xnr2j2

Russell, T., Helstrup-Alvarez, A., Allen, T., Evans, L., & Novick, R. (2016, January 25). Are we doing enough? Part 2: More tough questions we get asked about engagement practices and programming in the arts. [Blog post]. Read the full series at www.irvine.org/arts. Retrieved from https://medium.com/new-faces-new-spaces/are-we-doing-enough-part-2-bd5afea8e008#.7sgpw8qum

Schonfeld, R., Westermann, M., & Sweeney, L. (2015, July 28). *The Andrew W. Mellon Foundation: Art museum staff demographic survey.* New York: The Andrew W. Mellon Foundation. Retrieved from https://mellon.org/media/filer_public/ba/99/ba99e53a-48d5-4038-80e1-66f9ba1c020e/awmf_museum_diversity_report_aamd_7-28-15.pdf

The Harwood Institute for Public Innovation. (n.d.). Our approach: Turning outward. Retrieved from http://theharwoodinstitute.org/overview/

The James Irvine Foundation. (2014, October). *Emerging lessons and implications from the Exploring Engagement Fund.* Retrieved from https://irvine-dot-org.s3.amazonaws.com/documents/100/attachments/emerginglessonseef.pdf?1414714611

The James Irvine Foundation. (n.d.a). Arts engagement: Strengthening grantees. Retrieved from https://www.irvine.org/arts/who-we-fund

The James Irvine Foundation. (n.d.b). Arts engagement: Strengthening the practice, supporting the field. Retrieved from https://www.irvine.org/arts

The Wallace Foundation. (n.d.). The Wallace approach. Retrieved from http://www.wallacefoundation.org/how-we-work/the-wallace-approach/Pages/default.aspx

University of Kansas Work Group for Community Health and Development Community Tool Box. (n.d.). Section 5. Collective impact. Retrieved from http://ctb.ku.edu/en/table-of-contents/overview/models-for-community-health-and-development/collective-impact/main

University of Minnesota's Center for Spirituality & Healing. (2013). What is community wellbeing? Taking Charge of Your Health & Wellbeing. Retrieved from http://www.taking charge.csh.umn.edu/enhance-your-wellbeing/community/what-community-wellbeing. The Taking Charge of Your Health & Wellbeing website offers evidence-based information on health and wellbeing for individuals and communities.

Vogel, C. (2014, June 9). A new role for local libraries and museums. New York, NY: Local Institute for Comprehensive Community Development. Retrieved from http://www. instituteccd.org/news/5016

Walker, D. (2015, June 11). What's next for the Ford Foundation? [Blog post]. Retrieved from https://www.fordfoundation.org/ideas/equals-change-blog/posts/whats-next-for-the-ford-foundation/

W. K. Kellogg Foundation. (2016). WKKF leads a broad coalition to launch Truth, Racial Healing & Transformation process aimed at addressing centuries of racial inequities in the United States [Press release]. Retrieved from https://www.wkkf.org/news-and-media/article/2016/01/wkkf-leads-broad-coalition-to-launch-trht

W. K. Kellogg Foundation. (n.d.a). Community & civic engagement. Retrieved from https://www.wkkf.org/what-we-do/community-and-civic-engagement

W. K. Kellogg Foundation. (n.d.b). What we do. Retrieved from https://www.wkkf.org/what-we-do/overview

3

RELEVANT COMMUNITY THEORY

The concept of museums connecting with their communities is informed by several community-focused theories. These theories help museum leadership and staff understand why and how things happen in community-focused work, providing explanations for some of the phenomena and behaviors they observe. Chapter 2 focused on what role museums can play in building healthier communities. Chapter 3 highlights *why* this connection makes a difference and how it happens.

Peter Block: Creating Connections and Invitations

Peter Block's concepts of belonging and invitation are the underpinning for much of the content and practice described in this book. When leadership and staff create opportunities for belonging and invite people to join with them, they create and nurture the relationships that are part of community. These concepts are illustrated in many of the stories from the field described in later chapters. In *Community: The Structure of Belonging* (2008), he describes community in this way: "*Community* as used here is about the experience of belonging." For Block, community is based on a sense of feeling connected to others on a deeper level.

Block notes that community happens more easily in small groups:

> The small group gains power with certain kinds of conversations. To build community, we seek conversations where people show up by invitation rather than mandate, and experience an intimate and authentic relatedness. We have conversations where the focus is on the communal possibility and there is a shift in ownership of this place, even though others are in charge. We structure these conversations so that diversity of thinking and dissent are given space, commitments are made without barter, and the gifts of each person and our community are acknowledged and valued.
>
> *Block, 2008, p. 93*

Block also describes "the other": when someone perceives someone else as fundamentally different from themselves, the connections that bring people together are not as readily perceived.

Block notes,

> When we believe that the "other" is the problem and that transformation is required of them and not of us, we become the beneficiaries of their suffering in the world. Some of us make a living off of their deficiencies. We study their needs, devise professionals to service them, create institutions dependent on the existence of these deficiencies. All done with sincere intent and in the name of virtue.
>
> In our philanthropy, this mindset that the "other" is the problem means that we need to wait for them to change before the change we want in the world can come to pass. And until they change, we need to stay distant and contain them. This diverts us from the realization that we have the means, the tools, the thinking to create a world we want to inhabit, and to do it for all. If we saw others as another aspect of ourselves, we would welcome them into our midst. We would let them know that they belong, that they are neighbors, with all their complexity.
>
> *Block, 2008, p. 58*

The idea of "the other" means that someone focuses on what the *other* person needs to do or change. This idea of "the other" separates people, and it is harder to make connections. Block's description of what happens with "othering" is very helpful in understanding one's own internal assumptions and implicit bias and beginning to address them.

What does bring people together? When people connect to those who were previously strangers, when they invite people to join them in conversation, people connect. Block notes,

> [Communal transformation] occurs when we become related in a new way to those we are intending to help. This means we stop labeling others for their deficiencies and focus on their gifts. (Block, 2008, p. 60)
>
> The transformation we seek occurs when these two conditions are created: when we produce deeper relatedness across boundaries, and when we create new conversations that focus on the gifts and capacities of others.
>
> *Block, 2008, pp. 60,61*

For Block, *invitation* is crucial:

> Invitation is the means through which hospitality is created. Invitation counters the conventional belief that change requires mandate or persuasion. Invitation honors the importance of choice, the necessary condition for accountability. We begin with the question of whom do we want in

the room. For starters, we want people who are not used to being together. Then we include the six elements of a powerful invitation: naming the possibility about which we are convening, being clear about who we invite, emphasizing freedom of choice in showing up, specifying what is required of each should they choose to attend, making a clear request, and making the invitation as personal as possible.

Block, 2008, p. 113

Robert Putnam: Creating Trusting Relationships

Trust is based, in part, on actual experience; to create a trusting relationship one needs to understand the experiences of those with whom they want to connect. Highlighting the importance of building trust and deepening relationships is in turn highlighting social capital – increasing one's connections by doing things together. Robert Putnam in *Bowling Alone* (2000) and *Better Together* (2003, with Lewis M. Feldstein) describes social capital, the idea that social networks have value. Putnam notes that an important aspect of social capital is *generalized reciprocity* – when someone does something for someone else without the expectation that they will do something in return, but with the unspoken trust that they will do something when it's needed. The *pay it forward* notion is an example of generalized reciprocity.

Social capital – the bonds and relationships people have with one another – is as complex as the diversity of relationships that exist. Social capital is at the same time inclusive and exclusive. As Putnam notes, "it is important to ask how the positive consequences of social capital – mutual support, cooperation, trust, institutional effectiveness – can be maximized and the negative manifestations – sectarianism, ethnocentrism, corruption – minimized" (2000, p. 22). Social capital is expressed in different types of networks. Some are focused on *bridging* – inclusive networks that bring diverse people together; some are focused on *bonding* – deepening relationships among people who already have strong connections – and these are more exclusive. It is important to acknowledge the type of network desired so that the approach and process can be informed. Is the focus on bridging, bringing diverse people together with a common interest in building a healthier community, such as establishing a neighborhood park? Is it more focused on bonding, bringing long-term members together for a deeper relationship with one's organization? Each of these requires different processes.

Putnam also notes that reciprocity, honesty, and trust have direct bearing in one's communities. He notes that *trustworthiness* is the key – not that one personally knows and trusts every person in the community but that members know that overall the people in the specific community are trustworthy. He distinguishes between "thin trust" – the trust people feel for new acquaintances they meet in everyday circumstances – and "thick trust" – relationships that are "strong, frequent, and nested in wider networks." Museum–community involvement necessitates both kinds of trusts.

Trust is a complex notion, and Putnam notes,

> In virtually all societies "have-nots" are less trusting than "haves," probably because haves are treated by others with more honesty and respect.
>
> *Putnam, 2000, p. 138*

Putnam's idea of "haves" and "have-nots" is relevant to the idea of privilege – that advantages, such as access to higher education or housing, are available only to certain groups of people. Privilege is addressed in Chapter 2 (some funders specifically address it), and throughout this book readers are encouraged to be aware of how Putnam's ideas align with their understanding of privilege. How can one better understand the complexities of building trusting relationships with people who have varying levels of privilege? What does each person need to understand about their own privilege, and how privilege affects their museum, in order to build trusting relationships with community members?

Creating a Theory of Change

A theory of change is a planning tool to guide community change efforts. It explains how and why specific activities are expected to produce specific outcomes. In many cases, a theory of change is used similarly to the way that logic models or other strategic planning tools are used, and it focuses on how actions taken build on one another to create long-term change. For those interested in more fully involving their communities, a theory of change helps articulate what one wants to accomplish and how to plan. A theory of change model articulates underlying assumptions and provides explanations and justifications about why and how each activity (or precondition) needs to be met to move to the next goal.

Andrea A. Anderson, PhD, writing for the Aspen Institute Roundtable on Community Change, describes this:

> At its most basic, a theory of change explains how a group of early and intermediate accomplishments sets the stage for producing long-range results. A more complete theory of change articulates the assumptions about the process through which change will occur, and specifies the ways in which all of the required early and intermediate outcomes related to achieving the desired long-term change will be brought about and documented as they occur.
>
> *n.d., p. 1.*

Anderson also notes,

> We ask theory of change participants to predict exactly who or what is going to change, over what period of time, and by how much, at every single step in an often complex process. We ask them to specify how and why they expect change to happen in a particular way. We also ask how

> they are going to bring their resources to bear on creating early and intermediate changes that add up to their ultimate goal.
>
> *n.d., p. 3*

What does this mean in practical terms? To change, one has to know what they really want to change. For example, is the goal – what one wants to change – to increase the connections local neighbors feel with one's organization? Is it to have neighbors feel that one's organization is relevant and a valued community resource? Is the goal for local citizens to approve bond measures that support the organization's work? Is the goal to have a clean physical neighborhood? Using a theory of change model enables the group of stakeholders to create a map – a graphic image called a pathway of change – that illustrates the relationship between actions and outcomes. Every part of that pathway, including the intermediate outcomes, is a precondition to the long-term goal.

A theory of change is shown as a graphic image, which helps one see the big picture quickly – to look at what must be changed first to get to the next level. In this way, the focus is on identifying all the preconditions *before* focusing on how to accomplish them.

This example (Figure 3.1) from the Santa Cruz Museum of Art & History demonstrates how a theory of change model can inspire action.

An important element is identifying the indicators of success for each intermediate outcome (or precondition). How will one know that a specific precondition has been addressed? Consider what can be measured that would demonstrate success. For instance, the precondition may be "Families (with children under 18) from the local neighborhood utilize the museum's spaces at least once a month." This would be measured by collecting ZIP codes and group configurations of every visit, by reviewing which organizations bring groups of families and children, and through partnering with local youth- and family-serving organizations, such as YMCA, Boys and Girls Clubs, Scouts, and local community centers and church groups and arranging for special visits to the museum. Each of these methods provides an indicator and, taken together, they give a clearer idea of how close one is to attaining this intermediate goal.

Other sources of information that can be accessed to measure specific indicators include broader information, such as employment statistics, crime statistics, household data, community data, and statistics from schools. Consider which stakeholders have access to this information, and consider bringing them into the planning process. For example, partnering with local youth- and family-serving organizations also serves as an activity or program to accomplish this outcome, so it is not just an indicator (measuring the number of people and groups participating) but an activity as well.

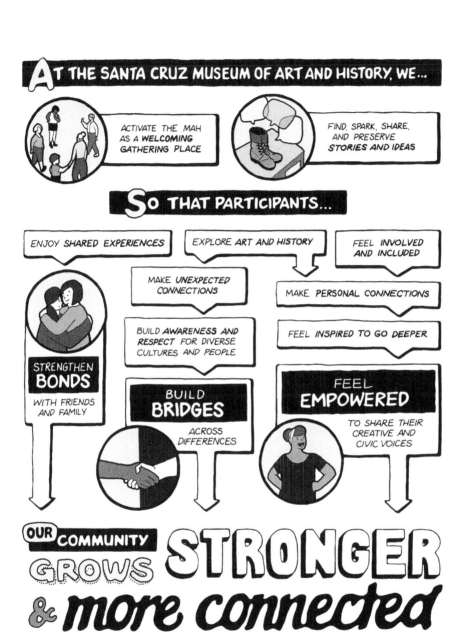

FIGURE 3.1 Example of a theory of change.

Courtesy of Santa Cruz Museum of Art & History.

Bibliography

Anderson, A. A. (n.d.). *The community builder's approach to theory of change: A practical guide to theory development.* New York: Aspen Institute Roundtable on Community Change. Retrieved from http://www.dochas.ie/Shared/Files/4/TOC_fac_guide.pdf

Block, P. (2008). *Community: The structure of belonging.* San Francisco: Berrett-Koehler.

Putnam, R. (2000). *Bowling alone.* New York: Simon & Schuster.

Putnam, R., & Feldstein, L. M. (2003). *Better together.* New York: Simon & Schuster.

Santa Cruz Museum of Art & History. (n.d.). *Theory of change.* Retrieved from https://santacruzmah.org/about/mission-and-impact/

4

MUSEUMS AND COMMUNITIES TIMELINE

A History

There has been a robust field-wide emphasis on museum–community involvement since the late 1980s, and this focus has been accelerating in recent years. These long-term efforts have significantly impacted the field, changing the way museum leadership and staff think about the role of museums as vital members of their communities.

In 1989, the American Association of Museums – now the American Alliance of Museums (AAM) – created the Task Force on Museum Education, which produced *Excellence and Equity: Education and the Public Dimension of Museums* in 1992. This publication was considered groundbreaking: the impetus for change as a seminal guiding document for the museum field. It outlines principles guiding museums in the process of becoming more public-service and community minded. It is a set of ten principles based on three key ideas: that education is central to museums' public service; museums must become more inclusive places; and dynamic, forceful leadership is the primary key to fulfilling museums' public-service role. The principles outlined in *Excellence and Equity* are powerful guidelines, but they are not specific in how museums can accomplish them. Many questions were raised as a result of the challenges raised in *Excellence and Equity*.

Developed concurrently with *Excellence and Equity*, AAM created MAP III, the Public Dimension Assessment, which focused on museums' public awareness/public perception, public participation/public experience, and public involvement. The intention of the Public Dimension Assessment was to provide a way for museums to better understand the implications of the document and to highlight the ways museums could begin to address and implement the recommendations presented in *Excellence and Equity*. This assessment has been adjusted in the years since it was adopted in 1991 and is now called the Community Engagement Assessment.

Museums' attempts to answer these questions led to many efforts to learn about the process of community collaboration. It also led to learning about assessing the

---

**BOX 4.1 KEY QUESTIONS PROVOKED BY THE AAM'S
EXCELLENCE AND EQUITY REPORT**

- How do museum leadership and staff develop working relationships with specific communities, especially when they don't know anyone in those communities?
- How does museum leadership assemble the staff and volunteers with the knowledge and skills to develop these relationships?
- How do museum leadership and staff involve representatives of various communities in the research and documentation process?
- How does the museum staff develop collaborative efforts? Collaborations are often complicated, and museum staff may be unfamiliar with effective ways to create and support collaborations.
- How does the museum leadership involve community advisory groups in decision making?
- How can museums be held accountable to be equitable in all their operations?

---

internal museum organization to see whether the museum was ready to take on the challenges of community work. Along with AAM, other museum organizations, such as the American Association for State and Local History, Association of Science-Technology Centers, Association of Children's Museums, and others, have focused on museum–community involvement for decades.

Community-focused initiatives, such as *Museums in the Life of a City: The Philadelphia Initiative for Cultural Pluralism* (1989–1992) and *Opening the Museum: History and Strategies Toward a More Inclusive Institution*, published by the Children's Museum, Boston, in 1993, describe the focus on creating inclusive organizations in Philadelphia and the decades-long focus on community involvement at the Children's Museum, Boston.

In 1994, Museum Management Consultants conducted research and wrote the *Bay Area Research Project: A Multicultural Audience Study for Bay Area Museums*. In 1997, AAM's Technical Information Service published *Museums, Trustees and Communities: Building Reciprocal Relationships*, by Daryl K. Fischer. This is a sampling of some of the initiatives that people in the museum field were undertaking in the late 1980s to 1990s.

In 1998, AAM created the Museums and Community Initiative to consider "the potential for dynamic engagement between American communities and their museums." The Museums and Community Initiative aimed to explore an expanded civic role for museums. Over the course of about nine months, from the summer of 2000 through the spring of 2001, AAM convened community dialogues in six cities throughout the United States. The participants in each dialogue included people from businesses, social service organizations, local government, cultural organizations, and museums. This initiative resulted in the 2002 publication *Mastering Civic Engagement: A Challenge to Museums*, edited by Ellen Hirzy. As Hirzy notes:

> Civic engagement occurs when museum and community intersect – in subtle and overt ways, over time, and as an accepted and natural way of doing business. The museum becomes a center where people gather to meet and converse, a place that celebrates the richness of individual and collective experience, and a participant in collaborative problem solving. It is an active, visible player in civic life, a safe haven, and a trusted incubator of change. These are among the possibilities inherent in each museum's own definition and expression of community.
>
> *American Association of Museums, 2002, p. 9*

In the years since 2002, a number of initiatives have brought museums together to share their efforts and learn from one another. Several of these initiatives published books about their work, yielding some of the most useful information in the field, such as *Urban Network: Museums Embracing Communities* (2003) and Partners for Livable Communities' publications *Culture Connects All* (2011) and *Stories for Change* (2012). Chapter 2 included examples of community-focused work that foundations are supporting. This foundational support has resulted in a number of relevant publications over the years. In 1998 and 1999, the Lila Wallace-Reader's Digest Fund produced *Opening the Door to the Entire Community: How Museums Are Using Permanent Collections to Engage Audiences* (1998) *and Engaging the Entire Community: A New Role for Permanent Collections* (1999).

Many initiatives have resulted in books and other publications that identify lessons learned and provide tools for effectively engaging in community work. Other books provide new perspectives and models for community work, including Lois Silverman's *The Social Work of Museums* (2010); Richard Sandell's *Museums, Society, Inequality* (2002); Gail Anderson's *Reinventing the Museum* (2012); and the writings of Elaine Heumann Gurian, who consistently pushes those who work in and with museums to engage with their communities in meaningful and enduring ways.

Professional journals, including the *Journal of Museum Education, Curator, Museum News* (now known as *Museum*), *Museums & Social Issues, Museum & Society, The Exhibitionist, History News, Dimensions*, and others have featured articles focused on museums connecting with their communities. A few of the earlier articles that provide a longer-term perspective include John Falk's "Visitors: Toward a Better Understanding of Why People Go to Museums" in *Museum News*, March/April 1998, and "A Framework for Diversifying Museum Audiences" in *Museum News*, September/October 1998; Lonnie G. Bunch's "Flies in the Buttermilk: Museums, Diversity, and the Will to Change" in *Museum News*, July/August 2000; Carlos Tortolero's "Museums, Racism, and the Inclusiveness Chasm" in *Museum News*, November/December 2000; and David Thelen's "Learning Community: Lessons in Co-creating the Civic Museum" in *Museum News*, May/June 2001.

Urban Network: Museums Embracing Communities

At the same time that AAM was engaged with its Museums and Community Initiative, the Field Museum in Chicago sought and secured funding from the National Recreation Foundation to convene a national consortium on increasing access for diverse audiences. This consortium, called Urban Network, included ten museums: the American Museum of Natural History; the Art Institute of Chicago; the Brooklyn Museum of Art; Exploratorium; the Field Museum; the Houston Museum of Natural Science; the Museum of Fine Arts, Boston; the Oakland Museum of California; the Science Museum of Minnesota; and Walker Art Center. The communications firm Amdur Spitz & Associates was engaged to spearhead and facilitate the network's process. From 2002–2003, the consortium met and shared their experiences and lessons learned as they engaged in community involvement initiatives at each museum. They produced a book in 2003 entitled *Urban Network: Museums Embracing Communities*, with examples, case studies, and useful tools.

The Urban Network consortium museums looked critically at the internal and external criteria for effectively embracing their communities, and they created a set of questions and tools to guide other museums as they consider and commit to fuller community involvement. The sections on Program Development Blueprint and Evaluation provide articulate and concise guidelines for planning for and evaluating community involvement. When museums utilize these guidelines to more fully engage their communities, they see increased engagement. The case studies are well organized, and each organization provides an example of how the project played out at their organization. Each case study includes a description of who the program serves, program objectives, an overview of the program activities, the overarching goals of the program, three key factors leading to community engagement, key resources needed, and measuring for success. The case studies provide articulate real-world examples of organizations, using the tools provided in Sections 3 and 4.

Magnetic: The Art and Science of Engagement

In 2013, *Magnetic: The Art and Science of Engagement* was published by AAM. Authors Anne Bergeron and Beth Tuttle launched a research effort in 2009 to "identify and study museums that had not just survived the last decade, but were thriving and growing in spite of the challenges." Bergeron and Tuttle's research revealed that museums that increased their audience and community engagement efforts or significantly invested in building personal relationships considered these aspects important factors in their organizations' successes. Bergeron and Tuttle developed a concept of a magnetic museum:

> Magnetic Museums are high performance organizations that deliver tangible cultural and civic value, and achieve superior business results through a commitment to service, engagement, and empowerment of others. They are distinguished by powerful alignment around a compelling vision and

the lasting bonds they create through meaningful experiences that enrich and strengthen their internal and external communities.

Bergeron and Tuttle, 2013, p. 9

Six museums are profiled in the book: Philbrook Museum of Art, Conner Prairie Interactive History Park, Chrysler Museum of Art, Children's Museum Pittsburgh, Natural Science Center of Greensboro, and the Franklin Institute. Examples of professional practice, and how this practice plays out internally and externally, illustrate the impact each of these institutions has in its community.

Bergeron and Tuttle identify six core practices of magnetic museums and devote a chapter to each – including examples. The six core practices of magnetic museums are: build core alignment, embrace 360 engagement, empower others, widen the circle and invite the outside in, become essential, and build trust through high performance. The core practice "become essential" speaks most directly to the premise of this book: "By increasing their relevance, responsiveness, and value in mission-related ways, they become more meaningful, useful, and pertinent to daily life in their communities. They recognize the importance of meeting real needs that reflect authentic community priorities. Magnetic Museums intentionally seek out and invest in the points of intersection between the institutional vision and the community vision." It is critical to recognize that all six core practices of magnetic museums work together to support one another, resulting in an institution deeply engaged with its internal and external communities.

A related perspective is provided by Bob Harlow, the author of *The Road to Results: Effective Practices for Building Arts Audiences* (2014) and *Taking Out the Guesswork: A Guide to Using Research to Build Arts Audiences* (2015), both published by the Wallace Foundation. These publications focus on audience development; many of their recommendations are helpful in developing relationships with communities. As illustrated in the accompanying infographic (Figure 4.1), Harlow has identified nine effective practices of audience-building programs: recognize when change is needed, identify the target audience that fits, determine what kinds of barriers need to be removed, take out the guesswork, think through the relationships, provide multiple ways in, align the organization around the strategy, build in learning, and prepare for success (Harlow, 2014, p. 5).

Blogs

Communication media focused on museum–community involvement have been proliferating in more recent years, highlighting the increased interest in the field and providing accessible platforms to explore this. One of the earliest and most prolific blogs that has addressed museums deepening their relationships with their communities is Nina Simon's Museum 2.0 blog, begun in 2006. Simon and her guest bloggers frequently explore the deeper connections museums have with their communities and how those might play out in the community and in the museum. Another blog that frequently explores the museum–community connection is

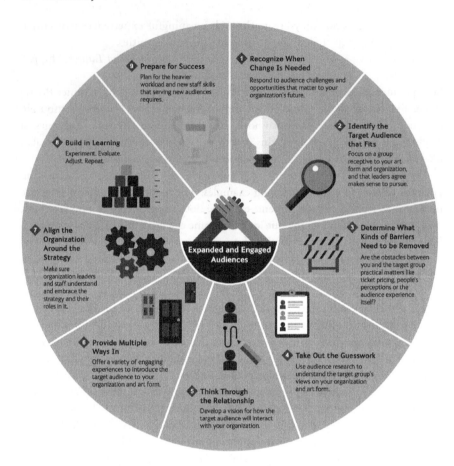

FIGURE 4.1 This infographic was produced by the Wallace Foundation based on the findings in *Effective Practices for Building Arts Audiences* by Bob Harlow.

Courtesy the Wallace Foundation.

Gretchen Jennings's Museum Commons blog, begun in 2011. Among the topics explored in Jennings's blog are The Empathetic Museum Project – "Creating a culture of commitment to community." The Incluseum blog, cofounded by Aletheia Wittman and Rose Paquet Kinsley in 2012, focuses on inclusive museum practices.

Museums Association

New research in 2016 from the British organization Museums Association is extremely relevant. As Jessica Turtle writes in *Valuing Diversity: The Case for Inclusive Museums,*

> Community is often talked about, but what does it actually mean for each of our organisations? In addition, there is an argument that by identifying

and engaging with people on the basis of a single characteristic we are reducing identity. Identity is extremely complex and made and remade constantly as people negotiate their lives.

Museums Association, 2016, p. 7

In addition, Turtle asks critical questions such as "Most museums now have mission statements which incorporate some element of inclusion, but how many leaders embody these values? Does our behaviour match the mission? This is required for a sustained culture change that goes beyond project funding, shifts to the institutional core and allows organisations to truly question and explore systemic inequalities" (Museums Association, 2016, p. 7).

It is clear from the work, writing, and practice of many colleagues over many years that there is a growing commitment and activism to more deeply involve museums and cultural organizations with their communities.

Bibliography

American Alliance of Museums. (n.d.). Assessment types: Community Engagement Assessment. Retrieved from http://www.aam-us.org/resources/assessment-programs/MAP/assessment-types

American Association of Museums. (1992). *Excellence and equity: Education and the public dimension of museums.* Washington, DC: American Association of Museums.

American Association of Museums. (1995). *New visions: Tools for change in museums.* Washington, DC: American Association of Museums.

American Association of Museums. (2000). Museums and community initiative: Community dialogues. Retrieved from http://www.aam-us.org/communitydialogues.htm

American Association of Museums. (2002). *Mastering civic engagement: A challenge to museums.* Washington, DC: American Association of Museums.

Anderson, A. A. (n.d.). *The community builder's approach to theory of change: A practical guide to theory development.* New York, NY: The Aspen Institute Roundtable on Community Change. Retrieved from http://www.dochas.ie/Shared/Files/4/TOC_fac_guide.pdf

Anderson, G. (2012). *Reinventing the museum.* Lanham, MD: AltaMira Press.

Association of Science-Technology Centers. Dimensions. Retrieved from http://www.astc.org/publications/dimensions/

Bergeron, A., & Tuttle, B. (2013). *Magnetic: The art and science of engagement.* Washington, DC: AAM Press.

Bunch, L. G. (2000). Flies in the buttermilk: Museums, diversity, and the will to change. *Museum News*, July/August, 32–35.

Curator: The Museum Journal. Retrieved from http://www.curatorjournal.org/

Empathetic Museum Project. Retrieved from http://empatheticmuseum.weebly.com/

Exhibition. Retrieved from http://www.aam-us.org/about-us/publications/exhibition

Falk, J. A. (1998). Framework for diversifying museum audiences. *Museum News* September/October, 36–39, 61.

Falk, J. (1998). Visitors: Toward a better understanding of why people go to museums. *Museum News*, March/April.

Fischer, D. (1997). *Museums, trustees and communities: Building reciprocal relationships.* Washington, DC: American Association of Museums.

Harlow, B. (2014). *The road to results: Effective practices for building arts audiences.* New York: The Wallace Foundation.

Harlow, B. (2015). *Taking out the guesswork: A guide to using research to build arts audiences.* New York: The Wallace Foundation.

Hirzy, E. (1992). *Excellence and equity: Education and the public dimension of museums.* Washington, DC: American Association of Museums.

History News. Retrieved from http://about.aaslh.org/history-news/

Incluseum blog. Retrieved from https://incluseum.com/

Journal of Museum Education. Retrieved from http://museumeducation.info/jme

Lila Wallace-Reader's Digest Fund. (1998). *Opening the door to the entire community: how museums are using permanent collections to engage audiences.*

Lila Wallace-Reader's Digest Fund. (1999). *Engaging the entire community: A new role for permanent collections.*

Museum. Retrieved from http://www.aam-us.org/about-us/publications/museum-magazine

Museum 2.0 blog. Retrieved from http://museumtwo.blogspot.com/

Museum Commons blog. Retrieved from http://www.museumcommons.com/

Museum Management Consultants. (1994). *Bay Area research project: A multicultural audience study for Bay Area museums.* San Francisco: Museum Management Consultants.

Museums Association. (2016). *Valuing diversity: The case for inclusive museums* [Report by Jessica Turtle]. London. Retrieved from http://www.museumsassociation.org/download?id=1194934

Museums & Social Issues. Retrieved from http://www.tandfonline.com/loi/ymsi20

Partners for Livable Communities. (2011). *Culture connects all: Rethinking audiences in times of demographic change.* Retrieved from http://livable.org/livability-resources/reports-a-publications/520-culture-connects-all

Partners for Livable Communities. (2012). *Stories for change.* Retrieved from http://livable.org/livability-resources/reports-a-publications/564-stories-for-change-

Philadelphia Initiative for Cultural Pluralism. (1992). *Museums in the life of a city: Final report.* Philadelphia: American Association of Museums.

Sandell, R. (2002). *Museums, society, inequality.* New York: Routledge.

Silverman, L. H. (2010). *The social work of museums.* New York: Routledge.

Spitz, J. A., & Thom, M. (Eds.). (2003). *Urban network: Museums embracing communities.* Chicago: Field Museum. Distributed by The University of Chicago Press. Retrieved from http://amdurspitz.com/about-us/resources/

The Children's Museum, Boston. (1993). *Opening the museum: History and strategies toward a more inclusive institution.* Boston: The Children's Museum, Boston.

Thelen, D. (2001). Learning community: Lessons in co-creating the civic museum. *Museum News,* May/June, 56–59, 68–73, 92, 94–95.

Tortolero, C. (2000). Museums, racism, and the inclusiveness chasm. *Museum News,* November/December, 31–35.

5

HOW OTHER COMMUNITY-FOCUSED FIELDS INFORM MUSEUM PRACTICE

Neighborhoods are always changing, and often a museum's perspective on its neighborhood is limited, which makes it hard to engage. Community-focused fields, such as public health, arts policy, and comprehensive community development, and fields focused on equity and inclusion have developed extensive processes for learning about communities. This chapter will explain how other sectors learn about and engage communities.

Public Health Sector

The public health field is deeply engaged with learning about communities to support healthier communities, and their processes can inform people in the cultural sector. Public health research is focused on ways to improve the lives of community members. This may look at ways to prevent diseases, such as diabetes, or ways to address environmental health issues.

A particular area of public health research called community-based participatory research engages community members as active participants in the research process. The publication *The Role of Community-Based Participatory Research: Creating Partnerships, Improving Health*, published by the U.S. Department of Health & Human Services Agency for Healthcare Research and Quality, notes:

In CBPR, community-based organizations (CBOs) or groups (such as churches, church members, neighborhood organizations, community residents, and other social organizations) help researchers to recruit subjects. But they do more than that. Community-based organizations play a direct role in the design and conduct of the research study by:

- Bringing community members into the study as partners, not just subjects.
- Using the knowledge of the community to understand health problems and to design activities to improve health care (interventions).

- Connecting community members directly with how the research is done and what comes out of it.
- Providing immediate benefits from the results of the research to the community that participated in the study.

In CBPR, community members are also involved in getting the word out about the research and promoting the use of the research findings. This involvement can help improve the quality of life and health care in the community by putting new knowledge in the hands of those who need to make changes.

Agency for Healthcare Research and Quality, June 2003

University programs in public health are a good place to start connecting with people who are already engaged with learning about specific communities. There may be people in these programs who are interested in working with museum leadership and staff to create community-focused programs that address cultural and health interests.

Race Equity/Inclusion and Arts Policies Sectors

The lessons from the field of race equity and inclusion provide a number of effective approaches to community involvement. PolicyLink is an economic development organization, based in Oakland, California and with a national scope, that helps build sustainable communities by advocating for equity to drive policy decisions. Jeremy Liu, the senior fellow for Art, Culture, and Equitable Development, shared his perspective about the role of arts and cultural organizations in promoting equity during a walking tour of selected Oakland arts organizations. With the walking tour, part of the Open Engagement art and social practice conference in 2016, Liu engaged participants in looking critically at arts organizations as playing a vital role in promoting equity.

The Oakland Museum of California (OMCA) was the first stop on the tour, and Liu spoke about the role of OMCA. Liu's commentary provides a critical lens through which to consider this work. He noted that in the arts and culture field, PolicyLink is very interested in ensuring that people who care about equity are equipped with the tools to accelerate their work. Institutions – large or medium-sized organizations that are not grassroots or community based – play a specific role in their local funding ecosystem. Liu noted that the Oakland Museum of California is an example. It is an institution that uses resources from the philanthropy and public sectors – resources that could otherwise potentially be used in different ways to support grassroots organizations. Midsize or large institutions like the Oakland Museum have opportunities for income that a grassroots cultural organization does not have. They need to grapple with how they create their annual budget so that it reflects an awareness of their role in the local ecosystem. (J. Liu, personal communication, April 29, 2016).

Liu's assessment provides a new perspective, one that enables museum leadership and staff to see the larger picture – to consider the ecosystem in which museums and cultural organizations operate. What role do midsize or larger organizations play in the local funding ecosystem? These organizations may be serving as community catalysts, as described in Chapter 2, so their role in the community may be very supportive. However, a more intensive look may reveal that midsize and larger organizations use a larger portion of available funding and that the funds that grassroots or community-based organizations are able to access are much more limited.

When assessing the overall health of the community, it is useful to look carefully at the vitality and health of *all* cultural organizations and for funders to pay particular attention to who they fund and *how* they consider the impact of each organization. Does the organization – whether it be large, midsize, community-based, or grass roots – address critical community concerns? What are the impacts of the organization's work? How deeply does a financial investment in an organization impact the people in a community? The answers to these questions will assist funders as they analyze funding opportunities and make equitable decisions.

In *Not Just Money: Equity Issues in Cultural Philanthropy*, Holly Sidford and Alexis Frasz look at how funding for the arts in the United States is getting *less* equitable. In most cities, a larger portion of funds is going to larger institutions, and smaller, community-based organizations are getting a smaller portion of the funding than they did just five years ago. Sidford and Frasz point out that many grassroots and community-based cultural organizations work in communities "compromised by long-term disinvestment by the public and private sectors, which has had rippling negative effects on the health, income, education, safety and other life circumstances of local residents" (Sidford and Frasz, 2017, p. 14). Because of this, community-based cultural organizations play an especially important role as a catalyst for community health and well-being. Sidford and Frasz also point out that community-based cultural organizations have a diminished capacity to generate contributed income and earned income, less access to grants of substantial size, diminished capacity to develop reserves and generate investment income, and fewer full-time staff members (Sidford and Frasz, 2017, p. 14). Bearing in mind these constraints, it is particularly important that midsize or larger cultural organizations and funders consider how to be more equitable in funding and supporting community-based and grassroots organizations.

What is equally important is to recognize that the practices that have led to this are rooted in the institutional, systemic biases that were part of most organizations' beginnings and continue to shape the organizations' internal culture. In the United States, cultural organizations have typically been founded based on Western European cultural values, which became embedded in their operations and are difficult to change. Museums and cultural organizations were often founded with gifts from wealthy donors and run in a top-down hierarchy. Cultural organizations espouse very different ideals in the twenty-first century, but the internal cultures of many organizations still reflect some of these outdated values, such as relying on staff who are willing to work at lower wages.

Additional lessons from the field of race equity and inclusion provide a number of effective approaches to community involvement. The Annie E. Casey Foundation's publication, *Race Equity and Inclusion Action Guide*, shows how learning about and incorporating a race equity and inclusion lens is impacting their work. The Action Guide highlights seven key steps to advancing race equity and inclusion in organizations:

Step 1: Establish an understanding of race equity and inclusion principles;
Step 2: Engage affected populations and stakeholders;
Step 3: Gather and analyze disaggregated data;
Step 4: Conduct systems analysis of root causes of inequities;
Step 5: Identify strategies and target resources to address root causes of inequities;
Step 6: Conduct race equity impact assessment for all policies and decision making;
Step 7: Continuously evaluate effectiveness and adapt strategies.

Step 2 is especially relevant. The excerpt below from the *Race Equity and Inclusion Action Guide* describes an equity-focused process that is useful for museums and cultural organizations as they become more involved with their communities:

Step 2: ENGAGE AFFECTED POPULATIONS AND STAKEHOLDERS

One of the impacts of systemic racialization is the exclusion of people of color from many avenues of decision making, civic participation and power. People of color, the most direct stakeholders in the elimination of racism and those with the most firsthand experiences with its effects, must have a role in social-change efforts along with whites. Strive to engage stakeholders who have active and authentic connections to their respective communities. It is important to ensure meaningful participation, voice and ownership. The sooner you can engage a diverse mix of stakeholders, the sooner you will be able to move from talk to action in creating equitable opportunities for the communities you seek to serve.

There is a difference between stakeholder engagement and empowerment. Engagement may simply involve getting input or limited participation. Empowerment involves taking leadership, making decisions and designing solutions and strategies at every phase of social-change efforts.

A community-organizing model led by people of color and focused on building power can be a particularly important strategy for advancing racial justice. Invest time in learning about the needs of the populations you are serving. Spend time understanding what other stakeholders are doing, examining what is working and then sharing the knowledge. This can help inform your work and allows early buy-in and support from the stakeholders and communities that you are serving. The sooner you can engage a diverse mix of stakeholders, the better. It is harder to bring new communities in once an organization has established its agenda, strategy and leadership. You can use a stakeholder analysis to assess whom you need on board to build a powerful mix of people to leverage change.

Stakeholder Analysis Guide

The following questions can help ensure you have a powerful mix of stakeholders to help leverage change.

1. Who is most adversely affected by the issue being addressed? Who faces racial barriers or bias, or exclusion from power, related to this issue?
2. How are people of different racial groups differently situated or affected by this issue?
3. Ideally, what would the racial composition of the leadership look like?
4. In what ways are stakeholders most affected by the issue already involved in addressing it? How can these efforts be supported and expanded?
5. What are ways stakeholders adversely affected by the issue can be further engaged?
6. How can diverse communities and leaders be engaged from the outset so they have a real opportunity to shape the solutions and strategies?
7. How can community engagement be inclusive, representative and authentic?
8. How will stakeholders exercise real leadership and power?
9. Who can be allies and supporters and how can they be engaged?
10. Who needs to be recruited or invited to join the effort to address this issue? Who will approach them? How? When? What will they be asked to do to get involved?

The Annie E. Casey Foundation, 2014, pp. 3, 6

The National Endowment for the Arts, recognizing the importance of bringing together health, research, and the arts, has published a useful guide for those in the health and arts sectors. *The National Endowment for the Arts Guide to Community-Engaged Research in the Arts and Health* provides guidance on how to partner effectively to document and assess how community-based arts programs are associated with positive health outcomes.

Education Sector

It is clear that numerous sectors are committed to building healthier communities, and local schools may often be involved in this process. A national initiative called Turnaround Arts is specifically addressing community engagement in schools. According to Michael Feldman, writing for the Createquity blog on October 13, 2015:

> Turnaround Arts is a whole-school initiative aimed at reforming the lowest-performing schools through intensive integration of arts and culture into classroom instruction and school life. Administered by Americans for

the Arts and overseen by the President's Committee on the Arts and Humanities (PCAH), an arm of the federal government, the initiative was implemented in eight schools around the country beginning in 2012. . . .

The Turnaround Arts program is built on eight strategic pillars, which include development of a "strategic arts plan," leadership from the principal and support from the school district and parents, at least forty-five minutes a week of dedicated arts instruction, integrating arts-based learning techniques into non-arts subjects, and collaboration with local arts groups.

. . . Turnaround Arts asks schools to consider the role of the arts in engaging parents, improving school infrastructure, and boosting the effectiveness of the administration's leadership – and it trains non-arts classroom teachers to integrate arts throughout the curriculum, even in those darlings of reformers, literacy and math classes. Schools have considerable latitude in how exactly they implement the model, but the overall theory is that the arts shouldn't be a bow pasted on education improvement or an occasional intervention in cordoned-off spaces; they should lie at the heart of how we help the schools and kids who struggle most.

Feldman, October 13, 2015

Feldman notes that the schools that participated in the Turnaround Arts initiative were selected based on their having strong school leadership and a committed school district, so they were ready. Readiness for engaging in community-based work will be addressed more fully in Chapter 6.

Comprehensive Community Development Sector

Comprehensive community development is a field that is directly relevant to museums and cultural organizations. The Institute of Museum and Library Services (IMLS) partnered with the Local Initiatives Support Corporation (LISC) to better understand how museums and libraries are working to support comprehensive community revitalization. LISC and IMLS focused on the ways in which museums and libraries are and can be crucial partners in community development efforts, making a measurable impact in communities.

Comprehensive community development encompasses housing, education, health, safety, economic development, employment, transportation, and community leadership. Working with colleagues in this field connects museum leadership and staff with others whose primary aims are building healthier communities and revitalizing neighborhoods. Examples of projects might include connecting with a CDC (Community Development Corporation) and community leaders to develop after-school programs for youth or working with a health organization to develop programs and activities for new mothers and their babies. Museums and cultural organizations, working with representatives from all these sectors, can be part of the team developing these programs.

Bibliography

Agency for Healthcare Research and Quality. (2003, June). *The role of community-based participatory research: Creating partnerships, improving health.* AHRQ Publication No. 03-0037. Rockville, MD: Agency for Healthcare Research and Quality. Retrieved from https://archive.ahrq.gov/research/cbprrole.htm

Chapline, J., & Johnson, J. (2016, December). *The National Endowment for the Arts guide to community-engaged research in the arts and health.* Retrieved from https://www.arts.gov/publications/national-endowment-arts-guide-community-engaged-research-arts-and-health

Feldman, M. (2015, October 13). White House artists in the school house: A new evaluation of the Turnaround Arts initiative shows promising results for underprivileged students [Blog post]. Retrieved from http://createquity.com/2015/10/white-house-artists-in-the-school-house/?utm_source=Createquity&utm_campaign=7d6caf688d-Createquity+email+blast&utm_medium=email&utm_term=0_05d97ced75-7d6caf688d-291090073

HOPE SF Learning Center. (n.d.). Health Equity Institute. Retrieved from http://healthequity.sfsu.edu/content/hope-sf-learning-center

Local Initiatives Support Corporation & Institute of Museum and Library Services. (2015). *Museums, libraries and comprehensive initiatives: A first look at emerging experience.* Retrieved from https://www.imls.gov/publications/museums-libraries-and-comprehensive-initiatives-first-look-emerging-experience

Museums Association (2016). *Valuing diversity: The case for inclusive museums* [Report by Jessica Turtle]. London. Retrieved from http://www.museumsassociation.org/download?id=1194934

PolicyLink. (2015). *The equity manifesto.* Retrieved from http://www.policylink.org/sites/default/files/pl_sum15_manifesto_FINAL_4app.pdf

Sidford, H., & Frasz, A. (2017, July). *Not just money: Equity issues in cultural philanthropy.* Retrieved from http://notjustmoney.us/docs/NotJustMoney_Full_Report_July2017.pdf

The Annie E. Casey Foundation. (2014). *Race equity and inclusion action guide.* Retrieved from http://www.aecf.org/resources/race-equity-and-inclusion-action-guide/

Bibliography

PART II

Creating a Community Involvement Action Plan

Knowing the terms to use, the history, and other sectors working in community involvement, a museum is now ready to focus on the practical aspects of involving museums in communities, with suggested actions and processes. The first step is taking an internal look at the organization, where readers will focus on learning about their museums and learning about themselves. The next step is learning about communities, creating a community profile, and creating a community involvement action plan.

Overall Planning

The goals of Part II are to give readers an understanding and tools to begin developing a plan of action for involving the community with the museum. Community involvement plans are aligned with the museum's mission and overall strategic plan if there is one.

In general, the focus is on *thinking strategically*, a process to help people make decisions. As the museum leadership and staff create the Community Involvement Action Plan, they will engage with fellow staff members to think about their answers to the following:

- What are our overall goals for this project (including addressing how the project aligns with the museum's mission)?
- Why do we want fuller involvement with the community?
- What do we specifically want to happen as a result of this project?
- Who will be responsible for managing/overseeing this project?
- What is the action plan (what strategies will we use to carry out this plan)?
- What resources will we need to accomplish this, and where will we get them?
- What is our timeline for this project and for the overall work?

- How will we measure our results? How will we know whether we've accomplished our goals, what we said we wanted to do?
- What information do we need (about our internal environment and our external environment) to set realistic and achievable goals? This may include:

  o   Who are our audiences?
  o   What is our niche?
  o   What do community members think about our programs and our museum?
  o   Who are our allies?
  o   What are the threats and/or barriers for this initiative?

When museum staff members think about and formulate answers for each of these questions, they are approaching their work strategically, and it becomes more compelling because they can say, with conviction, "This is what we do, this is why we do it, and these are our results." The planners guide this process.

6

LEARNING ABOUT THE MUSEUM AND LEARNING ABOUT ONESELF

Ellen Hirzy notes in *Mastering Civic Engagement*:

> Museums that are fully and imaginatively engaged in community have dynamic, risk-taking boards and staff leaders; committed staff who bring civic-minded values to museum work; and the ability to contend with ambiguity, reinvent conventional approaches, and learn from failure.
>
> *American Association of Museums, 2002, p. 10*

Intention: Why Involve the Community?

From the many experiences and stories illustrating museum–community involvement, it is clear that the work of building *internal capacity* is the first step. This is one of the most critical lessons in this book – *it is essential to be clear about why the museum leadership and staff are doing this, what internal capacity is in place, and what additional internal capacity may be needed.*

The staff may be excited to be launching into a museum–community involvement initiative and want to jump right into learning about the community. It is critical to harness that enthusiasm and begin by planning.

As museum leadership and staff begin to build internal capacity, they will need to consider *why* each step is taken. How does this specific action move the work forward? Each step one takes is a microcosm of modeling a new way of doing things – collaborative, built on trust and respect for one another.

A museum's community involvement work will be effective when the leadership and staff are *intentional* about what they do and when the museum is *ready to engage fully*. Deepening the museum–community relationship requires a high level of trust among museum leadership, staff, and community members. Trust is developed in part through sharing authority; the museum's leadership and staff welcome

---

BOX 6.1 KEY QUESTIONS ON INVOLVING THE COMMUNITY

- What is your intention for engaging in a museum–community involvement initiative?
- Why do you want to have stronger relationships with people and organizations in your community?
- What do you hope will happen as you become more fully involved in your community?
- How does increased involvement with your community align with your organization's mission, vision, and values?
- How do you plan to build your internal capacity so that, when you do begin to learn about your community, you have staff and capacity to act on what you learn?

---

community voices in the museum's programs and are included in the museum's day-to-day practice.

How will museum leadership and staff know whether/when their museum is ready to be more fully involved with its community? Consider these questions:

- What *indicators* – signposts that reveal readiness to share authority – are in place? Document the indicators and describe why each one indicates a readiness to share authority. What does authentically sharing authority look like for the museum and the community?
- How do the museum's leadership and staff *demonstrate* readiness to share authority? What internal and external processes are in place to support this readiness?
- How has the institution *prepared itself* to share decision making? This is different, but related to, sharing authority. A shared decision-making process may well be a precursor to sharing authority, and it can be practiced and honed internally. What practices has the institution embedded that support shared decision making? Is there institution-wide support for shared decision making?
- What does it look like for the organization to authentically share power? Institution-wide conversations can reveal much about the readiness of an organization to share authority and power.

Effective community involvement happens more readily when a museum:

- *Is aware of perceived power differentials*
  Do the museum's leadership and staff understand how they are perceived in the community? Do they understand and value the perspective of each community stakeholder they are working with, regardless of whether they are associated with a large organization, a small organization, or are an individual stakeholder?

How do they demonstrate that they value these perspectives? What are they doing to balance the power differentials?

- *Values and respects what every person and organization brings to the table*
Do the museum's leadership and staff fully value the unique perspectives that community members and organizations bring to the table? Are they considered as assets and not as issues, needs, or problems? Is each person's contributions valued and respected? How does the museum leadership and staff demonstrate that they value and respect community members' perspectives?
- *Shares authority*
Do the museum leaders and community leaders have an equitable and balanced decision-making process, and is it clearly articulated? Are the roles of each person and organization clarified, and are they equitable? There is much more involved in shared authority, and these are early questions to address on the path to museum–community involvement.

Jeremy Liu, senior fellow for Arts, Culture, and Equitable Development at PolicyLink in Oakland, California, notes that there are museums, such as the Wing Luke Museum in Seattle, that do share power and are core to the community's life and identity. *These museums act as an organizing mechanism for a community.* The power dynamic is vitally important. Institutions that receive hotel tax money from the public sector need to *demonstrate commitment to community power and influence.* Organizations need to understand, recognize, and embrace what influence and power they have (J. Liu, personal communication, December 21, 2016).

Internal Capacity

As museum leadership and staff begin to talk about the *intention* for increased involvement with their community, they will need to consider whether they have the internalcapacity to more effectively involve their communities. This work is time-intensive and requires sufficient staff time and energy to establish and nurture relationships over the long term. Is there enough staff bandwidth so that staff members can spend sufficient time in the community? This often means evenings and weekends, when neighborhood associations and other community groups meet, and it is important for museum staff to be present and active in these meetings. If the museum does not have sufficient staffing to accommodate this, it will need to move more slowly and on a smaller scale. Perhaps the leadership and staff can identify one or two people in their community to get to know better and nurture a relationship with them. As those relationships deepen, museum staff can slowly add more connections to develop and nurture.

Institutional Assessment

The beginning of the journey to embrace community involvement starts with a consideration and analysis of intention and internal capacity. These are part of the institutional assessment process, which looks at all aspects of an organization and assesses each area according to a number of criteria. An *institutional assessment* is an important first step in creating a plan for community involvement. It is a picture of the institution, past and present.

In an institutional assessment, staff and leadership collect and analyze many types of detailed information from throughout the institution, including attendance data, store sales, membership data, grants received, number and types of exhibitions and programs, staffing, board composition, marketing data, and many other sources of information. Institutional assessments are an essential part of understanding an organization. They show what past and present practices are and what the future may hold. The internal organizational environment is not the only focus; institutional assessments also look at and describe the external environment.

In conducting an institutional assessment, staff and leadership look at many types of information from the museum's website, past and current grant proposals and grant reports, past and present strategic plans, visitor research, members' surveys, and so on. Through an institutional assessment, museum leadership and staff are able to identify internal barriers, and they may also indicate what needs to happen differently for the organization to thrive. This is especially relevant as the museum seeks to become more fully involved with its communities.

When one is *learning* about their museum and conducting an institutional assessment, consider the following:

- *What can be learned* about an organization by reviewing its website? A website is often one of the first points of entry for someone to learn about the organization. What does your website say about you?
- *What can be learned* about an organization by reviewing its grant proposals? In a grant proposal, a museum presents its best self. What does the museum say about what matters to it?
- *What can be learned* about an organization by reviewing its attendance data? How does the museum collect this data, and what information does it collect? What is important for museum leadership and staff to know about the people who visit, and do the staff members have the tools to collect and analyze this information?
- *How do the museum leadership and staff think about audiences?* How do they identify and describe current audiences, including audiences served on-site and off-site?
- *What are the internal workings of the museum?* As the museum leadership and staff begin to develop a community involvement action plan, they will need to know more about every aspect of the organization. Who should be involved in creating and providing information?
- *How will the leadership and staff analyze the information* that they collect about their organization? What will they look for? Why might that information be important?

The answer to each of these questions reveals a great deal about the organization. For example, if an organization's website includes information about the organization's *processes*, it indicates that this is a more transparent organization. Websites that invite people to become involved in those processes (not just how to become a member but also how to propose exhibitions and become part of a community advisory group) are indicators of more inclusive organizations. Websites that include extensive information for people with disabilities indicate more inclusive and welcoming organizations. Examples include the Wing Luke Museum of the Asian Pacific American Experience, whose website includes descriptions of its community process, values, and principles; the San Francisco Public Library, whose website includes policies, guidelines, and forms for proposing exhibitions and programs; and the Contemporary Jewish Museum, whose website includes programs and services available for a range of abilities.

A review of a museum's grant proposals reveals a great deal about what is important to a museum's leadership and staff at a particular moment in time. Proposals to fund specific projects indicate where the museum is focusing its energy and what its intentions are. They reveal how strategic the museum is in its approach and how well the leadership and staff articulate their goals and intended outcomes. Organizations that do not clearly articulate goals, strategies, and intended outcomes may be less structured or linear in their approach. This does not mean that they are less effective in building relationships or involving their communities, but it does merit a deeper look into how the organization operates.

Reviewing attendance data reveals a number of things: How important is it to the organization to understand who attends? What information does it collect, and what does it do with this information? Does it regularly review and analyze this data, noting trends, raising questions about who is (and who is not) visiting, and considering how the answers to these questions impact its practice? Does it have the capacity and tools to collect additional information and use it to inform its practice? If it is collecting demographic information, what methods is it using, and are they appropriate? The answers to these questions provide an understanding of how nuanced the museum's understanding of its audiences are.

Reviewing the internal workings of the organization is a primary task, and it reveals a great deal about the organization overall. How inclusive is the internal culture of the organization? To what degree is community-focused work spread throughout the institution, and to what degree is it the responsibility of just one department? In conducting an institutional assessment, it is important to look at who is involved and who supports this work.

Planning for community involvement means identifying what makes one's organization unique, which is also part of the institutional assessment. A good place to begin a discussion about the museum's unique niche is to ask staff, board members, volunteers, community stakeholders, and members, "What do you consider to be the unique and distinctive characteristics of your museum?" This internal assessment process examines *the museum's unique role in its community* and establishes a foundation for strategic thinking about community involvement. When the museum's leadership and staff can articulate that – when they can say it in an expressive and significant way – they can communicate it effectively to their community. This will be an important part of the organization's community engagement.

The Reinventing the Museum Tool, from Gail Anderson's book *Reinventing the Museum: The Evolving Conversation on the Paradigm Shift*, helps frame the ideological shift in thinking over the past century.

> Within an institution, an illuminating dialogue can unfold using the Reinventing the Museum Tool to discuss where a museum currently stands in the continuum between the traditional museum and the reinvented museum and where it wishes to be. Issues about relevancy, institutional vitality, and alignment with contemporary museum practice can be discussed relative to a specific institution.
>
> *Anderson, 2012, p. 2*

The tool (Box 6.2) uses carefully crafted terms organized under two headings – traditional and reinvented – grouped in relation to institutional values, governance, management strategies, and communication ideology. Anderson's point with this tool is to spot-light the differences as a trigger to encourage museum boards and staff to examine their institutional stance in contemporary times. In a conversation with Anderson, she pointed out that many museums have never had this level of institutional examination before and find it illuminating and meaningful to have such an open dialogue. Some institutions have realized they are more in agreement than they previously thought, while others engage in a lively discussion over conflicting viewpoints. Further, Anderson points out, the goal isn't to be squarely in the reinvented column; rather, the goal is to be honest about where an institution is today and where it would like to be. It is about honesty, institutional reflection, capacity, and attentiveness to what an institution says it does and what its true convictions are.

Focused institutional assessments are very useful in looking more deeply and intentionally at a specific area of a museum's operations. Shining a light on a particular realm of museum work reveals themes and information that may not become evident in a more general overview. In the story below, a project at the California Center for the Arts, Escondido Museum, provided an opportunity to look with a focused lens at current and potential audiences.

Stories from the Field: An Example of a Focused Institutional Assessment

In 2010, the California Center for the Arts, Escondido Museum (CCAE), engaged in an audience development initiative to attract and serve adults ages 25 through 45. The audience development project was intended to gather information about this specific target audience, analyze the information gathered, and create a list of recommendations to attract and serve this audience. The CCAE includes a concert hall, a theater, a contemporary art museum, art and dance studios, and a conference center. The research process for the institutional assessment began with a preliminary analysis, with the intent to *benchmark* – to better understand where CCAE was at the starting point for this study, where it had been, and how it arrived at this point in time, including past and present practices.

In conducting a focused institutional assessment, the audience research team had many questions and sought an extensive amount of information to get as clear an understanding of the institution as possible. They requested the following information from the staff – information which would be used to inform the preliminary audience development assessment:

Audiences

- Information about visitors to the museum (for the prior two years).

  o Number of visitors, ages of visitors, where they came from (ZIP codes), ethnicity (if visitors voluntarily provided this information), group configurations (families with children, adult groups, etc.).

- Information about visitors/audiences at CCAE *overall* (including the concert hall, theater, studios, and conference center) (for the prior two years).

  o Number of people, ages of audience members, where they came from (ZIP codes), ethnicity (if visitors voluntarily provided this information), group configurations (families with children, adult groups, etc.).

- Information about museum members.

  o Membership categories, how many in each category, ZIP codes for each category, age and ethnicity of members (if members voluntarily provided this information).

- Information about current members at CCAE (concert hall, theater, studios, and conference center).

  o Membership categories, how many in each category, ZIP codes for each category, age and ethnicity of members (if members voluntarily provided this information).

- Information about who participates in museum programs.

  o Number of people who had attended programs in the prior two years (list by the different types of programs), ages of audience members, where they came from (ZIP codes), ethnicity (if program participants voluntarily provided this information), whether the attendance at programs is increasing, staying the same, or decreasing.

Marketing

- Marketing budget.
- Number of people on the marketing staff.

BOX 6.2 REINVENTING THE MUSEUM TOOL

This tool is an excerpt from *Reinventing the Museum: The Evolving Conversation on the Paradigm Shift,* edited by Gail Anderson and published by AltaMira Press in 2012. It is revised from the 2004 first edition.

The Reinventing the Museum Tool captures the essence of the paradigm shift occurring in museums. The terms on the left depict the assumptions and values that capture traditional museums. The terms on the right illustrate the characteristics typical of the reinvented museum. Museum trustees and staff are encouraged to use this tool to clarify where a museum stands in the continuum between the traditional museum and the reinvented museum and where it wishes to be. This can trigger discussions about relevancy, institutional vitality, and responsiveness appropriate to a changing world. Each museum will determine which qualities of its operation to retain and which new approaches to adopt in support of an intentional direction. This institutional reflection may trigger varying levels of change and transformation for a museum.

TRADITIONAL MUSEUM	REINVENTED MUSEUM
Institutional Values	
Values as ancillary	Values as core tenets
Institutional viewpoint	Global perspective
Insular society	Civic engagement
Social activity	Social responsibility
Collection-driven	Audience-focused
Limited representation	Broad representation
Internal perspective	Community participant
Business as usual	Reflective practice
Accepted realities	Culture of inquiry
Voice of authority	Multiple viewpoints
Information provider	Knowledge facilitator
Individual roles	Collective accountability
Focused on past	Relevant and forward-looking
Reserved	Compassionate

TRADITIONAL MUSEUM	REINVENTED MUSEUM
Governance	
Mission as document	Mission-driven
Exclusive	Inclusive
Reactive	Proactive
Ethnocentric	Multicultural

TRADITIONAL MUSEUM		REINVENTED MUSEUM
Internal focus	....	Expansive perspective
Individual vision	....	Institutional vision
Single visionary leader	....	Shared leadership
Obligatory oversight	....	Inspired investment
Assumed value	....	Earned value
Good intentions	....	Public accountability
Private	....	Transparent
Venerability	....	Humility
Caretaker	....	Steward
Managing	....	Governing
Stability	....	Sustainability

Management Strategies

Inwardly driven	....	Responsive to stakeholders
Various activities	....	Strategic priorities
Selling	....	Marketing
Assumptions about audiences	....	Knowledge about audiences
Hierarchical structure	....	Learning organization
Unilateral decision making	....	Collective decision making
Limited access	....	Open access
Segregated functions	....	Integrated operations
Compartmentalized goals	....	Holistic, shared goals
Status quo	....	Informed risk taking
Fund development	....	Entrepreneurial
Individual work	....	Collaboration
Static role	....	Strategic positioning

Communication Ideology

Privileged information	....	Accessible information
Suppressed differences	....	Welcomed differences
Debate/discussion	....	Dialogue
Enforced directives	....	Interactive choices
One-way communication	....	Two-way communication
Keeper of knowledge	....	Exchange of knowledge
Presenting	....	Facilitating
Two-dimensional	....	Multidimensional
Analog	....	Virtual
Protective	....	Welcoming

Courtesy AltaMira Press.

- Skills, knowledge, and experiences with specific marketing techniques among the staff: There are many avenues for people to learn about events and programs in the community, and the more diverse skills the staff has, the more effective the organization will be in motivating people to engage with the organization. Knowing this information helps leadership and staff clarify the resources available to communicate with priority audiences.
- Brief description of marketing strategies.
- Whether the museum sends electronic newsletters and to whom.
- Whether they collect names and email addresses at programs and events and what they do with this information.
- What they know about their website visitors, including how many people visit their website and how people use the website.
- What social media they are active in and how they are collecting and using the data from their social media activities.
- What marketing materials are printed, how the printed materials are distributed, and to whom they are sent.
- A description of their relationships with journalists, bloggers, podcasters, and other people in the media.
- Whether they have tracked where their visitors or program attendees hear about them and what they have learned from this.
- Whether they offer discount coupons, how they track redemption of these coupons, what the outcome of discount coupon programs has been, whether the effort has been sustained, and how the discount coupons have been publicized.

Outreach/Specific Audiences

- Description of any past efforts to engage with specific audiences.
- When the specific outreach activities occurred.
- Description of the specific priority audience.
- Outcome of each outreach effort, whether it has been sustained, why it has or has not been sustained, and what museum staff and leadership have learned from the experience.

Description of any community partnership projects

- Which organizations and why the museum partnered with those specific organizations.
- When the partnership projects were initiated and whether they have continued and are sustainable.
- Assessment of how strong the relationships with the community organizations are and whether museum staff and leadership continue to keep in touch with the organizations even if the specific project ended.

Focus Geographic Area

- Description of the priority geographic area for this project.
- Whether the priority geographic area is residential or mixed business/residential.
- Description of the demographics of the residents of this area (average age, household income, number of households with children under 18, race and ethnicity, etc.).
- Description of the community groups in this geographic area that serve the museum's priority audience.

Programs

- Description of the programs currently offered by the museum.
- Description of other programs offered in the past four years.
- Description of the priority audience for each current program.
- Number of participants in programs for the priority audiences.
- Description of past programs for the priority audiences, including their current status, whether they were discontinued, and, if so, why they were discontinued.
- Description of whether the museum worked with any community groups in planning/publicizing past programs for priority audiences.

Additional information requested

- Any previous visitor studies and previous program evaluations for the museum and for the center.
- Grant proposal narratives about the museum and its audiences.
- Brochures about the museum and its programs.
- Annual reports.
- Visitor comments.
- Information about the community.

The information requested by the audience research team was extensive and may have looked overwhelming at first, but it provided an in-depth understanding of the organization at the beginning of the project. This illustrates how a focused institutional assessment can be a useful tool in planning for community involvement. In the case of CCAE, it provided a baseline picture of the organization and its practices to date, allowing the audience research team to understand much more about the CCAE's internal and external work. The focused institutional assessment revealed key findings about the museum's history and its interactions with its various constituencies, public awareness and public perception of the museum, its relationship with the city of Escondido, and the ways in which other arts organizations are serving CCAE's priority audiences. It also revealed key findings about the internal practices of the museum, including marketing goals and plans, an overview of the number of exhibitions and related attendance, an overview of the museum's audiences and programs, and a description of the museum's community partnerships. Taken together, these findings brought to light several primary issues and questions that would be explored further through a survey. They included questions about the primary aspects that are important in making decisions about activities and what barriers and constraints might stop young people from visiting the museum. The focused preliminary assessment of the institution also provided suggestions for how to more precisely consider priority audiences, how to leverage current programs, and how to consider community partnerships.

Continual learning about one's organization can lead to profound changes, as is shown in the following examples from the Oakland Museum of California and the Arab American National Museum.

Stories from the Field: Oakland Museum of California

The Oakland Museum of California (OMCA), a multidisciplinary museum highlighting the art, history, and natural science of California, is deeply engaged in community work and exemplifies best practice in significant ways. Chapter 5 shared the perspective of Jeremy Liu from PolicyLink about OMCA. Kelly McKinley, OMCA deputy director, describes how the museum is considering and engaging its community and how OMCA is looking internally as well as externally, focusing on its impact in the community. McKinley notes that this is not a straight path and it takes time, commitment, and work:

> Our work in community engagement really started in earnest just over ten years ago with the arrival of Lori Fogarty as the Museum's Director and CEO. We started by asking, "What does it mean to be a visitor-centered museum?" Guided by intense community consultation, evaluation and prototyping, we spent the next several years reimagining the visitor experience across all of our galleries and incorporating the stories, voices and input of Oakland residents and organizations. We then asked "What does it mean to be a great neighbor?"– a question that took us and our programming outside of our four walls, meeting and talking to neighbors at community events and festivals. Now our question is "What does it mean to be an institution *in service to the people of Oakland*?" We are exploring what constitutes the real and demonstrable impact we can have on the quality of life and wellbeing of residents in this city.
>
> In the last two years we have come to terms with the fact that to be a great museum that serves the whole state, we need to be a great *Oakland* museum first. So we have been focusing on community engagement and audience development in a hyper local way. We focus on lifting up the stories of the people but in a way that connects to issues and ideas that affect people across the state and even the nation. We need to be a beloved Oakland institution before we can even begin being connected and relevant to the rest of the state. We have focused our "playing field" to precisely 44 ZIP codes –

the ZIP codes of people who live in the East Bay and under an hour's drive to the museum. Imagine concentric circles: There are 44 ZIP codes in the biggest circle, 22 ZIP codes in the next one in, and 4 ZIP codes in the circle immediately around the museum. These are the most economically disadvantaged and under-resourced communities in Oakland – Fruitvale, West Oakland, Chinatown, and Downtown. We are focusing on each of these circles in very particular ways.

As we think more about the ways we serve our community, we are also thinking more about the ways we operate as part of an ecosystem of organizations that serve the wellbeing of Oakland residents. What does it mean for us, in conjunction with all the other civic and non-profit organizations, to work together to make living in Oakland better for all people? What is, ultimately, our desired social impact? What precisely is the difference we make in the lives of citizens? What is our unique contribution to the social wellbeing? How might we think about our unique contribution amplified and complemented by the contributions of other organizations that occupy our civic ecosystem? We are working with a consultant from PolicyLink here in Oakland who is helping us to hone in on what we can uniquely claim as our contribution, our impact.

Starting about a year ago, we began to work out our Theory of Change, working with a basic logic model: We do these kinds of activities, which generate these kinds of outputs or programs, which have these kinds of outcomes for people, with this kind of ultimate impact in the community. We are trying to chart a pathway to change. That was our first step to being much more intentional about a change agenda and achieving demonstrable social impact.

In addition to creating a road map, we have been growing our internal capacity to engage with community in new ways through cultural competency training with multiple cohorts of staff, across all levels of the organization. We have worked with an Oakland-based group called Leaderspring to build the techniques, skills and understanding to connect with the diversity of people living in Oakland to build a more relevant, equitable and inclusive organization. For example, this training has required us to examine our privilege as individuals and as an organization – more precisely, to examine the privilege of occupying seven acres of land in the heart of the city, with beautiful gardens, extensive real estate and vast collections of our cultural, natural and artistic heritage. All of those assets are things we can bring to the table in new ways to serve our community needs and interests. We are about to embark on a major fundraising campaign, and one of the cornerstones of that campaign is reimagining our gardens and campus – how we might "break the box" of the walled museum and create a public square - a place for gathering and connecting with our neighbors, the City and Lake Merritt.

We are also engaged in a series of conversations grappling with what relevance means. For us, it's about convening people in conversation about ideas that matter. Doing that requires us to adopt a different stance as an organization – to take a stand and not shy away from difficult, messy topics. Through our cultural competency work, we understand that there's a role for us to play in addressing issues of exclusion and race, and creating opportunities for people to have a greater sense of connection, not just to their community, but to people in their city, their neighbors. What that means is a different kind of exhibition program and a different kind of public program – programs that connect the stories of our past to our present, to equip and inspire people to more actively imagine a different kind of future for themselves, their families and their communities. Case in point are two exhibitions from our 2016/17 exhibition calendar: *Altered State: Marijuana in California* and *All Power to the People: Black Panthers at 50*. These were two very different kinds of exhibitions and experiences for our visitors but they both were conceived and designed to serve as a platform for people to come together to explore issues that have shaped and are shaping who we are as a community, to explore perspectives different from their own. All these things are connected. It hasn't been a straight path.

One example is how we develop exhibitions. Even though the museum has worked in a highly collaborative way for a very long time, it was still understood as a curatorial-led project. Now we are looking at how we make room for different kinds of leadership and conversations. How can we harness dissonance or disagreement productively toward achieving our goals? How can we give the staff language to voice concerns or critiques in a way that doesn't feel personal? These are skills and situations that will support the important and difficult work we need to do to change as an organization. We are also making community engagement part of everybody's job. Much of the work I'm describing here has been supported through the Irvine Foundation's New California Arts Fund.

We are looking deeply at impact in the community and in the museum. A great example is the story of the development of our exhibition *Altered State: Marijuana in California*. We were working with Kathy McLean who is an expert in prototyping exhibition ideas. On one of our Friday Night events we covered all the walls of the café with butcher paper, and wrote and drew our ideas for the exhibition. We invited our Friday Night attendees to join us and let us know what they thought. We were happily surprised at the length of time people spent with our roughly collaged and Sharpie diagrammed content ideas, many in excess of an hour! We found people eager to share their ideas and perspectives on the direction of the show both in writing, drawings and, most significantly, in conversation with staff. Kathy McLean said, in all of her decades of prototyping, that she had never seen engagement and conversation at such a high level. What is causing this engagement? How can we describe what's happening for visitors, and how might we measure it? Figuring this out will be key to achieving our social impact goals and sustaining our organization.

At OMCA, community engagement means all the ways that people come to be in contact and conversation with us. We often talk about the Three Cs – our framework for understanding the spectrum of ways that we engage community in creating experiences at the Museum. The Three Cs are *contributing* ideas and voice, *collaborating* with us in a focused way, such as in a task force or an advisory committee, and *co-creation* where we make things together with community.

Community engagement is part of everybody's job. It is one of our four institutional values, and it's at the top of every job description. Community engagement is a priority in our strategic plan, and annual departmental and individual goals are designed to support those priorities. We also offer staff opportunities to volunteer in the community on paid time, so there is a whole spectrum for ways that people can be involved. We have been surveying the whole staff on an annual basis to track their understanding of and commitment to community engagement over the years. Much of our staff training is designed around community engagement, and every staff meeting includes a segment on community engagement.

We need to be able to articulate our value and our impact in a way that people in other sectors can understand. Doing so will enable us to partner with greater clarity and efficiency to achieve and amplify our goals and impact. Doing so will enable us to bring new kinds of partners and investors to the table and the cause.

K. McKinley, personal communication, April 8, 2016

OMCA is an excellent example of an organization that is committed to learning and adapting as it strives to involve its community more extensively. Among the most significant questions that McKinley asks are "What does it mean for us, in conjunction with all the other civic and non-profit organizations, to work together to make living in Oakland better for all people? What is, ultimately, our desired social impact? What precisely is the difference we make in the lives of citizens? What is our unique contribution to the social wellbeing? How might we think about our unique contribution amplified and complemented by the contributions of other organizations that occupy our civic ecosystem?" McKinley acknowledges the deep internal questioning about OMCA's role in the ecosystem of Oakland's civic and nonprofit organizations and the value of using a theory of change model to frame these questions and articulate the museum's social impact. For OMCA, this focus has intensified in the past two to three years, and it is enabling the museum to make significant changes in its internal operations.

A noteworthy change that OMCA is making in its internal operations is through cultural competency training. This is enabling the staff members to embrace a culturally competent stance in all their work. The University of Kansas's Work Group for Community Health and Development Community Tool Box notes, "A culturally competent organization brings together knowledge about different groups of people – and transforms it into standards, policies, and practices that make everything work." It further notes that the five principles of cultural competency are valuing diversity, conducting cultural self-assessment, understanding the dynamics of difference, institutionalizing cultural knowledge, and adapting to diversity (University of Kansas Work Group for Community Health and Development Community Tool Box, n.d.) With this training and support, OMCA staff members are increasingly able to learn and incorporate the attributes of cultural competency noted above, acknowledge the complexity of cultural identity, examine their privilege, and become more able to recognize the dynamics of power.

It is important to note that community involvement is not a brand new area of interest for OMCA but rather a continuation and intensification of the museum's focus on community. Working with organizations such as PolicyLink and Leaderspring is providing OMCA with the tools and skills to embed community involvement deeply in the organization. It will be very interesting to hear more from the other civic and nonprofit organizations that are part of OMCA's civic ecosystem as time goes on, to more clearly see how this vision and theory of change materializes over a number of years.

The Arab American National Museum, like the Oakland Museum of California, is committed to learning and adapting as it strives to serve its community more extensively and courageously address its challenges.

Stories from the Field: Arab American National Museum

The Arab American National Museum in Dearborn, Michigan, brings the voices and faces of Arab Americans to many audiences. The museum is committed to dispelling misconceptions about Arab Americans, and it is deeply involved in community work. According to Devon Akmon, director of the museum, leaders can sustain a strong community-focused culture at their museums through commitment to working with the community and building trust. Akmon notes that this deep commitment changes the entire approach of an institution and it must be a shared vision, done collaboratively.

The museum's focus on community started from its inception. The museum opened in May 2005, and while it was being developed, the founding director, Dr. Anan Ameri, traveled the country, engaging with Arab American communities, asking them, "What would you like to see in a museum? What would our nation's first and only museum dedicated to our culture look like?" As Akmon notes, "That was the true formation of our DNA, and I think that the most important aspect of that is ongoing engagement at all levels and at all times with our community, trying to be truly responsive to the needs of our community" (D. Akmon, personal communication, August 31, 2016).

These stories illustrate how museums are deeply engaged in reflecting on themselves as organizations. They illustrate how leaders recognize the attributes that are components of success. These attributes will be explored more thoroughly below, but it is appropriate to provide a short description of the leadership attributes that support community work here: flexibility; being open to and supportive of a creative, iterative process; being supportive of experimentation and knowing that sometimes things won't work the way one thought they would; patience; and commitment for the long term – in short, creating a supportive environment for one's community focus to grow and evolve.

Learning About Oneself: Key Attributes and Skills That Support Community Involvement

As the leadership and staff are learning about their museum and the attributes that support *organizational* community involvement, they will learn about the *people* who make up the museum – the staff, board, volunteers, members, visitors, and other stakeholders. They will also learn about their own individual characteristics, and that is a crucial part of this process. Leadership and staff will learn about their own attributes and identify the skills and attributes that are critical to effective community involvement. They will consider and connect with their own core competencies, knowing themselves and what they each do well. As they do this, they will be able to identify additional competencies, attributes, and skills that they need to add personally and to their staff, and they will be able to play to their strengths. The attributes and skills explored here will help to connect in vital ways with one's communities, external and internal.

Examining and Paying Attention to One's Assumptions

As noted in Chapter 3, Peter Block's *Community: The Structure of Belonging* examines notions of "the other." When someone perceives another person as fundamentally different from oneself, they do not see the connections that bind and they don't have empathy. The attribute that helps one understand oneself is the ability to look at one's own preconceived ideas and pay attention to one's own assumptions and unconscious biases. Self-reflection is the key – when people are able to articulate their own assumptions, they are able to understand how those assumptions influence what they think and how they approach their work. For example, do they assume that the people who live in a particular neighborhood are low-income? Is there an assumption that a particular community is primarily interested in exhibitions that relate to their cultures or backgrounds and not to anything else that the museum has to offer? How do those assumptions affect the actions before, during, and after an exhibition that may have particular interest for a specific community? Do the staff and leadership make connections with members of this community before and during the run of this exhibition and then stop connecting with them after the exhibition closes, assuming that they aren't interested in other things that the museum does? When people assume something, they reduce the opportunity to connect deeply and learn wholeheartedly.

Paying attention to and articulating one's assumptions is a skill that is used in planning as well. It is an integral part of the theory of change and strategic planning processes. When staff members and leadership articulate their assumptions, they explain *why* they think the proposed actions will bring about the specific outcome. It also helps people plan effective research and evaluation strategies. When staff and leadership are in the process of learning about a community, acknowledging their assumptions helps them to develop evaluation strategies that diminish the biases these assumptions may bring to the study. As an example, perhaps staff members are interested in learning more about the people who are residents of senior communities in their town so they can work more closely with them to provide services. What assumptions are staff members making about the seniors? Are there nuances about cultural groups that they need to know?

Understanding one's unconscious biases is especially challenging – how can a person pay attention to something if they are not conscious of it? Unconscious biases are a much deeper level of assumption and impact how someone feels, thinks, and behaves. It is relevant to bring it up in this context because unconscious biases may affect how museum staff and leadership do their work. See the Fear and Courage section below for an additional perspective.

Wholeheartedness

Among the most important attributes needed to support community involvement is wholeheartedness – being sincere, fully committed, and embracing all the emotions one has when one opens their heart to others. When one is wholehearted, one is also vulnerable. Wholeheartedness means caring deeply about what one is doing, being willing to be vulnerable as well as to do things differently. When one is wholehearted in community, one feels that the connections they make with others are necessary and core aspects of their life and work.

Wholeheartedness requires fully believing that one's connections and relationships are vital to their health, not only as an individual but also as a community and an organization. Dr. Parker Palmer, founder of the Center for Courage & Renewal, identifies pillars for living fully and wholeheartedly:

> Be passionate about some part of the natural and/or human worlds and take risks on its behalf, no matter how vulnerable they make you. Offer yourself to the world – your energies, your gifts, your visions, your heart – with open-hearted generosity. But understand that when you live that way you will soon learn how little you know and how easy it is to fail.
>
> As you integrate ignorance and failure into your knowledge and success, do the same with all the alien parts of yourself. Take everything that's bright and beautiful in you and introduce it to the shadow side of yourself. Let your altruism meet your egotism, let your generosity meet your greed, let your joy meet your grief. Everyone has a shadow. . . . But when you are able to say, "I am all of the above, my shadow as well as my light," the shadow's power is put in service of the good. Wholeness is the goal, but wholeness does not mean perfection, it means embracing brokenness as an integral part of your life.

> As you welcome whatever you find alien within yourself, extend that same welcome to whatever you find alien in the outer world. I don't know any virtue more important these days than hospitality to the stranger, to those we perceive as "other" than us.
>
> *Palmer, 2015*

Palmer's description captures the essence of wholeheartedness, a core attribute of authentic and meaningful connection.

Humility

> It is unwise to be too sure of one's own wisdom. It is healthy to be reminded that the strongest might weaken and the wisest might err.
>
> *Mahatma Gandhi*

Humility acknowledges that everyone has a distinct and valued point of view and the collective points of views are empowering. In many cases, others are more authentic and appropriate to speak to an issue. Humility means believing and acknowledging that "I am not the most important person." When someone embraces humility, they let go of ego and focus on others.

Humility plays out in a variety of ways, and relationships with community members can be significantly affected by others' perceptions of one's humility. When people think about themselves, do they consider themselves knowledgeable, experienced, and with important perspectives to bring to their relationships and community partnerships? Does this concept affect how they present themselves? Might they come across as being the expert? If so, then they are not exhibiting humility, and those with whom they are interested in working may not want to work with them. If it seems that people think of themselves as knowledgeable, it could well also seem as though they do not truly acknowledge and value the knowledge, perspectives, wisdom, experiences, and expertise of those with whom they want to connect.

We learn humility from world leaders, such as Nelson Mandela (2010): "There is a universal respect and even admiration for those who are humble and simple by nature, and who have absolute confidence in all human beings irrespective of their social status" (p. 406).

Humility does not mean that people do not have self-confidence. They may well be knowledgeable and experienced and have important perspectives to bring to their relationships and community partnerships. It is the way one communicates that is important. Humility is expressed when the people with whom one is connecting feel that they are being honored and valued for their knowledge, perspectives, wisdom, experiences, and expertise.

Fear and Courage

Museum leadership and staff may be apprehensive about reaching out, getting to know people, and developing relationships with people whom they perceive as different from themselves. When people embrace humility and vulnerability, they enter into discomfort. People are often afraid – afraid of getting their feelings hurt, afraid of saying the wrong thing, afraid of saying something insensitive – or worse, saying something offensive. How can people be sensitive to others but not be overly sensitive and afraid of having their feelings hurt? This requires courage, to be afraid of something and do it anyway.

Museum leaders and staff may be fearful of meeting with resistance from community members, of having their intentions questioned by community members. They may fear that their efforts will be met with skepticism, especially if they are not already part of a particular community. In actuality, museum practitioners who are deeply engaged in museum–community involvement indicate that there may have been a few relationships that were initially met with skepticism but *their commitment to the relationship* meant that over time this skepticism disappeared and the relationships developed and flourished. Their wholehearted commitment meant that their connection didn't come across as arrogance, insensitivity, or tokenism.

Patience and Tenacity

Patience is an attribute that is particularly effective in museum–community work. Change takes time, and patience supports an individual's ability to sustain that change. According to Earl Lewis, president of the Andrew Mellon Foundation, speaking during the *Diversity: From Talk to Action* session at the American Alliance of Museums annual meeting in May 2016, staying the course over an extended period of time yields results that would not be possible if the program were to end earlier. The Andrew Mellon Foundation's fellowship program, the Mellon Mays Undergraduate Fellowship Program, has existed for over twenty-five years. Lewis notes that if the fellowship program had ended after ten or fifteen years its impact would have been very different; the fellowship has had a compounding effect over those twenty-five years, building a pipeline that would not exist if the program had ended earlier (Lewis, 2016).

It is sometimes a struggle to be patient, to let things play out over the long term and in their own time. A person may want to take specific action steps to get something done, but developing relationships and involving community are ongoing. There is no ending date on these processes, and to approach work with an end in mind makes it harder to be patient. Patience means letting go of the urgency to adhere to a specific timeline and letting go of the sense that a specific action has to take place by a specific date.

Practicing patience means letting things unfold in ways that may not be clear at the outset. For example, staff members from a museum may be working on a collaborative project with community members. Perhaps this team meets once a week over a number of months; many of the conversations are about what the team might want to do or what they could do. The focus over these months is on talking, listening, and exploring possible ideas. It is not focused on reaching a decision and creating an action plan to implement that decision. For people who are focused more on action, practicing patience in this scenario may be looking at what they can do to assist this group process. Perhaps they can take notes during each meeting and share them with all the participants. Practicing patience means stepping back and finding what one *can* do to assist the group without being the driving force.

One aspect of patience bears special note: recognizing when it is more app-ropriate to work from the background and to foreground other voices and perspectives. This is when acknowledgment of privilege means consciously staying in the background and opening the space for other voices and perspectives to be more visible and foregrounded. Privilege, and how it impacts museum–community work, is explored more thoroughly later in this chapter and in Chapters 2 and 3.

Empathy

In Chapter 1, empathy – the ability to understand and share the feelings of another – was described as a core value embedded in the life and work of museums deeply involved in their communities, and it is an attribute of community-centered museums. Museum staff members who practice empathy focus not only on their own thoughts and feelings but also on understanding the thoughts and feelings of others. This approach is described by the Empathic Museum:

> The qualities of 21st century museums are impossible without an inner core of institutional empathy: the intention of the museum to be, and be perceived as, deeply connected with its community.
>
> [J]ust as empathetic individuals must have a clear sense of their own identities in order to perceive and respond effectively to the experience of others, the empathetic museum must have a clear vision of its role as a public institution within its community. From this vision flow process and policy decisions about every aspect of the museum – audience, staffing, collections, exhibitions and programming, social media, emergency responses – all the ways in which a museum engages with its community(ies).
>
> *Empathetic Museum, n.d.*

In practice, empathy may be expressed in a number of ways. When museum staff members are interested in connecting with community members, they research ways to connect and find that there are neighborhood groups and associations that meet on a regular basis. Museum staff members contact the neighborhood associa-tion organizers and are told that they are more than welcome to attend the next meeting, and a couple of staff members do so. While they are there, they listen to the concerns of the neighbors and gain a greater understanding of some of the neighbors' concerns and interests. Empathy in this instance helps the staff better understand the interests, concerns, and perspectives of others. It means that the staff members listen to the neighbors' concerns with openness, leading to their greater understanding of those concerns.

The Ability to Truly Listen

Truly listening is at the core of one's work with internal and external communities. How do people know when they are truly listening, and how do they develop and practice this skill?

Specialists in this area include Sondra Thiederman, PhD (engaged listening); Transforming Violence (eloquent listening); and Sakyong Mipham Rinpoche (true listening). These specialists focus on respecting and valuing others – important aspects of all one's relationships. They note that, when people truly listen, they:

- Attend – they focus on what the person is saying, not on what they will say in response. They turn their phones to silent and put them away. They don't pick them up, even to check messages, until the conversation is finished.
- Acknowledge their own assumptions. Assumptions create a filter, making it more difficult to hear the intentions of the speaker.
- Value and enjoy a diversity of perspectives.
- Have a genuine desire to learn about someone.
- Seek to understand the content and feeling of the message.
- Are patient – they let speakers develop their ideas. Even if they think they know where speakers are going, true listening means that they are not in the driver's seat – the speakers are.
- Empathize.
- Assume the other person has valuable things to offer.
- Ask clarifying questions – "Tell me more." When people ask someone to tell them more, they are letting the person know that they are paying attention and want to understand more fully.
- Ask the people they are with "What questions do you want to be asked?" This provides a welcoming, open-hearted invitation for people to say what's important to them and lets them know that the other person truly wants to know (Rinpoche, 2015; Thiederman, 2014; Transforming Violence, n.d.).

Examining these concepts reveals why they are important aspects of true listening. *Attending* also means paying attention and removing distractions. *Acknowledging their own assumptions* helps listeners to intentionally set them aside. For example, listeners might assume that speakers will be very interested in collaborating with them. This assumption might lead to misunderstandings, which in turn would hamper the process of building a trusting relationship. Setting aside expectations and assumptions helps listeners to hear and understand more clearly. *Valuing a diversity of perspectives* also includes appreciating what speakers bring to the table. When listeners value the diverse perspectives of speakers, they listen more openly. This does not necessarily mean that they agree with everything speakers say, but it does mean that they value speakers' perspectives. *Having a genuine desire to learn about people* is an aspect of wholeheartedness.

One way to embrace this is to remember a time when someone truly listened to you and remember how it felt that the listener was really paying attention. They were engaged with what you were trying to communicate. That sense of value is what museum leadership and staff strive to bring to their relationships. True listening is a skill that facilitates relationships internally, with one's staff, board, and volunteers, and externally, with one's communities. When people truly listen, they let other people know that they value their perspectives and their time together and that what they say matters.

True listening means preparing the way to be fully engaged in a conversation. Distractions abound, for listeners and their conversation partners. Listeners can set the scene for effective communication by asking, "Is now a good time to talk?" This signals that they would like to engage in a meaningful conversation, one where both people are focused and paying attention.

The tenets of dialogue provide a framework through which to understand and practice true listening. A dialogue is a focused and intentional conversation, not a discussion or debate, and it is guided by a set of principles:

- Seek to learn
- Suspend assumptions
- Speak from your own individual perspective and experience
- Suspend judgment – listen without judging
- Honor confidentiality
- Listen for understanding
- Ask clarifying and open-ended questions
- Honor silence and time for reflection
- One person speaks at a time

Lindahl, n.d., adapted from United Religions Initiative

True listening takes practice. When it is done wholeheartedly, listeners will see their relationships deepen and grow over the long term. And that is at the core of museums creating strong connections with their communities.

Paying attention

Paying attention is related to true listening in that it means focusing – reducing or eliminating distractions – so that one is present and focused. When people are paying attention, they are *attending to* someone or something, and they are more fully aware. They are able to perceive and understand the nuances of the experience. When people are with other people and paying attention, they notice more. What are their companions' voices like? What is their body language saying? When people are paying attention to their surroundings, they will notice more. What is it like walking through different neighborhoods? Are there any parks? Where are they? What do the schools look like? Does it look like this neighborhood has many or few resources? The more people pay attention, the less they will operate on autopilot and the more they will learn.

Being an Ally/Accomplice

The core of this work is developing and nurturing trusting relationships person to person, and expanding those relationships so that one's organization is infused with many trusting relationships with community members, stakeholders, and organizations. How do museum staff and leadership build that trust? By having all the attributes listed above and being an ally/accomplice. Much has been written in recent years about what being an ally or accomplice entails, including posts and articles published by Everyday Democracy, Racial Equity Tools, Colorlines, and others.

In 2014, video blogger Franchesca Ramsey outlined five tips for how to be an ally: understand your privilege; listen and do your homework; speak up, not over; apologize when you make mistakes; and do the work (Ramsey, 2014). A number of these tips relate to attributes already described above and provide succinct ways to practice them in daily life. In other words, an ally works *with* people, with humility. An ally asks, "How can I be helpful to you?"

Considerations for Staffing

In addition to learning about oneself and the skills and attributes that facilitate community involvement, museum leadership will also want to consider the skills and attributes that are critical to effective community involvement *within the organization,* among the staff and volunteers. Some of these skills and attributes were discussed in Chapter 1's focus on core values. They include respect, empathy, and true listening. Others were discussed earlier in this chapter – wholeheartedness, humility, and courage. Additional skills and attributes that are important for overall community involvement include the following:

- *Following through*
  When staff and volunteers at one's organization connect with community members, perhaps to learn more about the community, perhaps to begin talking about the possibility of partnering on a project, following through is an aspect that can make or break a project. It is related to the attributes of patience and tenacity already discussed, but there are some differences. It means being thorough – paying attention to the details and acting on them. Who needs to be contacted, and what does one need to do to make sure that everyone is notified/invited/welcomed? What questions are asked, how does one find out

the answers, and how does one communicate those answers to the appropriate people? How does one think through the details of their time together and create an atmosphere of trust? What can one do to let people know that they have been heard, that one is paying attention and following through?

- *Being present*
  This attribute is about the courage to go into the community and listen, many times – to be present. It is like true listening and paying attention, but it also includes the act of being physically present in the community. An example from the Grace Hudson Museum & Sun House in Ukiah, California, illustrates this: In March 2008, the Grace Hudson Museum & Sun House was hosting the exhibition *Sing Me Your Story, Dance Me Home: Art and Poetry from Native California*. The exhibition, organized by the California Exhibition Resources Alliance (now known as Exhibit Envoy), included works by more than thirty California Indian artists and poets exploring themes of family history, cultural heritage, and contemporary life. The museum's executive director, Sherri Smith-Ferri, and her staff planned a series of programs to accompany the exhibition. One program was a panel discussion on Life, Learning and Education, moderated by Malcolm Margolin and including Frank LaPena, Julia Parker, Sylvia Ross, L. Frank Manriquez, and Dugan Aguilar as participants. Part of the conversation focused on talking about how Margolin, the publisher of Heyday Books, was always present at local Native events. The trust that was built over time was palpable. As Theresa Harlan, who curated the exhibition, notes,

> As a former exhibitions director at the San Francisco-based American Indian Contemporary Arts (AICA) gallery, I still remember the way Malcolm Margolin established a relationship with AICA. He became a constant attendee at our events and eventually became a long-time friend. Malcolm approached us and told us he thought our work was wonderful and wanted to know more about us as an organization. As he became a familiar face, our exchange of information increased and we discovered we shared a wide California Native network. He didn't approach us with an agenda or immediate need.
>
> *Smith Kliebe, 2010, p. 3.*

This commitment to being present, to showing up, is illustrated in many of the stories in this book and in the day-to-day lives of exemplary museum leadership and staff.

- *Implementing these skills and attributes in work situations*
  The skills and attributes described above have immediate application in work situations. When one is meeting with community members, welcome and invite ideas, thoughts, and perspectives from all. Turn to each person and ask what they think. Sum up the discussion, making sure that everyone understands what each

person will do and when. Be willing and committed to spend the time and resources needed over the long term. Be intentional – choose to connect, choose to be authentic. Be open and ready to engage, and be accountable.

How does one sustain a community focus throughout? Much depends on who someone is at their core and what values their organization collectively holds. Staffing with a community focus is especially effective when done with community organizers – people who understand and have experience with grassroots organizations and organizing community members. Community organizers have on-the-ground expertise in bringing people together for a purpose. That purpose might be to develop and build a neighborhood playground or to organize people to protest, with the intention of influencing policy and practice. For the museums that embrace and do this, the impacts – internally and externally – are far reaching.

The Queens Museum in New York has been hiring community organizers for many years. Prerana Reddy, director of Public Programs & Community Engagement, shares more about this:

> We have been trying to focus on things that are meaningful for our neighborhood. We have a process of dialogue and a process of listening, talking with community members and asking questions – "What is a museum? What kinds of things do community members want?" We're looking not just at the museum itself, but how the museum can be in community spaces, such as libraries, community-based organizations, and other places where people already go. We asked, "What are the changes the community would like to see? What assets and networks could the museum bring to bear on this?" We wanted to hire a community organizer, someone familiar with the neighborhood, who could find out what community members are already doing or wanted to be doing.
>
> When Tom Finkelpearl came on as director in 2002, he was very interested in how to create this bridge with the community. He created a new department whose goal would be to generate collaborative programming, and hired community activists as museum staff. Sometimes, community activists didn't already have knowledge about contemporary art, so we provided this training. The Museum has continued to hire people with various experiences and backgrounds beyond art history or arts administration. At the Queens Museum, community work is everybody's job, not just those with "community" in their title. Experimentation is supported, with the idea that we'll figure it out together. We have a sense of safety here.
>
> *P. Reddy, personal communication, October 1, 2015*

In seeking to hire staff experienced in community organizing, the Queens Museum demonstrates that it values the expertise that community organizers bring to the table. This expertise and the perspectives that community organizers nurture within the institution have had an impact over many years. As Reddy notes, embedding community throughout the institution is demonstrated by (and accompanied by) a sense of experimentation and safety. All these elements – valuing community organizing expertise, a sense of experimentation, and a sense of safety – are attributes of a flexible and community-engaged organization. In Chapter 10, readers will see a specific example of how embracing community organizing expertise has changed the Queens Museum over the long term.

The Wing Luke Museum of the Asian Pacific American Experience (the Wing) in Seattle highlights the stories of the Asian Pacific American experience. The Wing is recognized for its community-based and community-driven exhibitions and programs. This value of community is at the heart of the Wing, infusing the culture of the organization. The Wing hires people skilled in community organizing, a practice it has been implementing since 1991 when community organizer and journalist Ron Chew was hired as executive director. As a community organizer, Chew had built and nurtured trusting relationships with many community members. People already knew and trusted him, paving the way for the museum's success in engaging the community. Fulfilling the Wing's mission required the museum to broaden the skills of its staff and turn away from more traditional methods of recruitment. Position descriptions and recruitment methods were redefined to include community organizing and negotiation. New staff members have come from the community, with skills nurtured in American ethnic studies and social justice movements. At the time, Chew noted, "Museums of the future need to look for staff . . . who are bridge-builders, have strong negotiation skills, and who can work collaboratively."

The focus on hiring from the community has had a tremendous impact on the Wing's ability to delve deeper into community concerns. Cassie Chinn, deputy executive director at the Wing, notes that there has been an impact on the organization and in the community on a number of different levels. Hiring individuals directly from the community provides the opportunity for staff members to develop their own skills and grow professionally. Over many years, the museum has seen that this investment in the community leads to increased community trust in the museum. Community members see the museum in a different light – as a place where they could work and have a career. Museum work is not among the traditional professions that immigrants and refugees generally consider, and the Wing's long commitment to hiring from the community changes this perspective. One outcome is a museum–community relationship that has grown and is thriving over the long term. Relationships are based on trust and understanding; community members know the families and the background of the staff members, so trust is built in from the beginning.

Accountability is also a critical component of the connection. Community members know that they have an avenue and a voice in the museum. When community members are hired as staff, the staff members know they have an additional level of accountability to community members. As one staff member noted, "I know I'm not on the right path [when I do something at the museum] if I get a call from my grandmother!" There is an increased sense of responsibility to the community.

With staff rooted in the community, the museum focuses on community concerns and perspectives and on how it can work alongside these. The Wing sees its role as a facilitator of community empowerment, growth, and capacity. As Chinn notes, "We want to make sure that we never take for granted the amount of trust it takes for community members to share their time, voice, and perspective with the museum – and their willingness to have the courage, generosity and strength to join with us" (C. Chinn, personal communication, April 11, 2017).

When the internal cultures of museums embrace and support the work of community organizers, these cultures are changed, and community is embedded in the internal culture. The voices of community organizers who understand the mechanisms of change are pushing the field to do so. As a result, activism has made its presence much more visible in the field in recent years. From #museumsrespondtoferguson to Museum Workers Speak to Museum Hue, voices in the field are saying loudly and clearly, "We must be heard!"

Specific skills that community organizers bring to the table include the ability to motivate people to participate, mobilize volunteers, analyze data to inform action, and build strong connections and relationships with community members. Jeremy Liu, senior fellow for Arts, Culture, and Equitable Development at PolicyLink in Oakland, California, notes that community organizers have an understanding of power dynamics – of institutional and community power and how it is generated and how it can be used. It is an understanding of how relationships that respect those dimensions are created. Liu explains that the role of an organizer can help museums have a relationship with their communities in a way that is hard for them to do otherwise. This is different from the role of doing community outreach and engagement because the *role of an organizer is to support and empower the community members* to help them shape their own lives and communities. And that is related to the power dynamic in a museum context.

How does one find people who have community organizing skills? Liu notes that peers, such as the staff and leadership at the Queens Museum and the Wing Luke Museum, are often very helpful. It is also helpful to connect with organizers who understand the arts and culture world generally, such as the Art x Culture x Social Justice Network (http://artculturejustice.com/), Alternate Roots (https://alternateroots.org/), Appalshop (https://www.appalshop.org/) in Appalachia and rural America, and Springboard for the Arts (http://springboardforthearts.org/) (J. Liu, personal communication, December 21, 2016).

Community organizers understand how people in community organizations work and the types of conversations that will lead to developing trusting relationships and partnerships with cultural organizations. They also understand how to help create a culture of valuing community within an organization.

Creating an Inclusive Work Environment

How can museum leadership and staff support people with valued skills after they are hired and working at a museum? As Jessica Turtle writes in *Valuing Diversity: The Case for Inclusive Museums*, for people who may identify as

... being of a diverse background, the day-to-day experience of working in museums can be exhausting and can present regular emotional and psychological challenges. This may lead to people leaving once they approach mid-career level, rather than continuing in a challenging landscape. In order to navigate organisational cultures, people report needing to: constantly articulate and demonstrate how they have achieved their position on merit; explain issues of identity and cultural heritage to colleagues and deal with micro-inequities on a daily basis. Micro-inequities occur as an effect of unconscious bias and can be defined as micro-messages that communicate who is "within" and who is "without". They are social and professional slights that can become collectively acted out without people realising. They have the effect of damaging morale and devaluing individuals. Although there have been some excellent entry route programmes to diversify the sector in recent years, there is anecdotal evidence that retention at mid-career level is an issue, due to the factors explored above.

Museums Association, 2016, p. 14

Turtle notes that

... research from the Equalities Challenge Unit demonstrates that unconscious bias not only impacts decisions related to recruitment and salary of individuals but also impacts investment in their ongoing development once inside an organisation.

Museums Association, 2016, p. 13

What's especially important is the "effect this has on day-to-day experience for those self-identifying as – or who are identified as – diverse" (Museums Association, 2016, p. 13).

Gretchen Jennings, who writes the Museum Commons blog, has highlighted "The Rule of Three" – the idea that when there are three or more people of diverse backgrounds in a group, the group culture begins to change – as a way to support staff of diverse backgrounds. She notes,

Just imagine what might happen if professional associations like AAM (including its Professional Networks), ASTC, ACM, AASLH, and various regional associations, our museums and other cultural organizations, our museum studies programs, etc. adopted The Rule of Three as an operative ideal for achieving institutional diversity and inclusion. Just think about the impact that three (or more) senior managers from underrepresented groups in our field might have on the organizational culture of our various institutions. It's not that three such people will think alike – far from it – but it's likely that business as usual (some might call it white privilege*) will be disrupted. This may be why the idea is a bit discomfiting – but worth considering.

★"... invisible systems conferring dominance on my group ... an invisible package of assets that [white people] can count on cashing in each day ... Conditions that are viewed by whites as morally neutral. normative, and average, and also ideal, so that when we work to benefit others, this is seen as work that will allow them to be more like us." Peggy Mcintosh. 1990.

Jennings, 2016

Supporting staff members who have come through nontraditional pathways and/ or are of a diverse background is a key aspect of creating a culture of valuing community so that they feel supported and do not feel as though they are doing the heavy lifting in creating an inclusive, community-centered organization. What does this support look like in a museum or cultural organization? There are a number of ways this is demonstrated.

Those who come through traditional pathways and/or are not of diverse backgrounds can support their colleagues by *educating themselves* on the issues of diverse communities, not relying on colleagues from diverse backgrounds to raise their awareness and educate them, which is a burden. There are many sources of information, including blogs and websites, that provide valuable perspectives about diverse communities and the role that museums and cultural organizations play, from Museum Hue to Visitors of Color to The Incluseum, just to name a few. More sites are included in the bibliography at the end of this chapter.

Canada's HR Council for the Nonprofit Sector provides guidance for creating an inclusive and supportive work environment: **"Open, effective communication, as well as clear channels for feedback** optimizes the opportunity for discussion of issues related to inclusion and discrimination. . . . Diversity and inclusion is best nurtured in an open workplace where mistakes can be used for learning – not for embarrassing or shaming individuals" (Canada's HR Council for the Nonprofit Sector, n.d.). Other tools available to guide museum leadership and staff include the publication *Diversity at Work: Creating an Inclusive and Supportive Work Environment*.

One of the primary challenges for effective community involvement currently is the dependence of this work on champions and specific people. When one of these champions leaves an organization, how do the museum leadership and staff continue to evolve and nurture their community relationships? This challenge will be addressed in Chapter 8, but this is a good place to acknowledge and recognize the importance of *everyone* embracing this work so that organizations do not find themselves in this position.

Full community involvement does not happen because specific positions, individuals, or roles are focused on community. In a community-involved organization, the culture of involvement should infuse every staff and volunteer position so that everyone in the organization supports the community-focused work of the museum. Infuse each staff and volunteer position description with language that supports this, including appropriate tasks and responsibilities, and staff members will understand more clearly what is expected of them and how each position has an important role to play in involving the community. There are guidelines available to assist in creating inclusive position descriptions, including those from CompassPoint and the University of Wisconsin Office of Equity, Diversity and Inclusion. See the bibliography at the end of this chapter for more information.

Pathways to Entry

What are the pathways for entry to become a museum professional, and how do these pathways limit access to people with valued community-based skills? There has been a great deal written about the traditional pathways leading to museum work and the challenges that are built into these traditional pathways – expecting/ requiring advanced degrees, low pay scale, high student debt, and unpaid/low paid internships. Focusing on these traditional pathways may limit access to people with other valued skills. There are a number of places where someone might find people with community-based skills, including people who have a background in urban studies, planning, and ethnic studies. A web search on urban studies will reveal several resources, including local colleges and universities with programs and degrees in urban studies as well as the organizations with which they work.

One can also find people who are skilled in community organizing by paying attention to the media. What organizations are working on local or regional community change in one's area? Who are the people who are coordinating those efforts? These may be the people with whom leadership and staff want to connect, who may be partners in community-focused projects. As the museum staff members get to know these community change coordinators and their colleagues, they will be connected with other people who are knowledgeable and skilled in community activism, and when the museum has position openings, they may be able to connect with people they already know, who have community organizing skills, to help fill the openings or refer them to others whose skills would add to the organization's skill set. One example of an organization that blends community activism with culture is A Blade of Grass (ABOG), whose focus is nurturing socially engaged art. See Chapter 8 for more about A Blade of Grass and its resources about planning for community partnerships.

Bibliography

#museumsrespondtoferguson. (n.d.). [Twitter feed]. Retrieved from https://twitter.com/hashtag/museumsrespondtoferguson

American Association of Museums. (2002). *Mastering civic engagement: A challenge to museums.* Washington, DC: American Association of Museums.

Anderson, G. (2012). *Reinventing the museum: The evolving conversation on the paradigm shift.* Lanham, MD: AltaMira Press.

Beckwith, D., & Lopez, C. (n.d.). *Community organizing: People power from the grassroots.* Retrieved from http://comm-org.wisc.edu/papers97/beckwith.htm

Brown, B. (2010, June). *The power of vulnerability* [Video file]. TEDxHouston. Retrieved from http://www.ted.com/talks/brene_brown_on_vulnerability.html

Cambridge Dictionary. (n.d.). Humility. Retrieved from http://dictionary.cambridge.org/us/dictionary/english/humility

Canada's HR Council for the Nonprofit Sector. (n.d.). Diversity at work: Creating an inclusive and supportive work environment. Retrieved from http://hrcouncil.ca/hr-toolkit/diversity-supportive-environment.cfm

Colorlines. (n.d.). Retrieved from https://www.colorlines.com/

Contemporary Jewish Museum. (n.d.). Accessibility. Retrieved from https://www.thecjm.org/accessibility_information

Dictionary.com. (n.d.). Wholehearted. Retrieved from http://www.dictionary.com/browse/wholehearted

Empathetic Museum. (n.d.). Retrieved from http://empatheticmuseum.weebly.com/

Everyday Democracy. (n.d.) Retrieved from https://www.everyday-democracy.org/

Goodreads. (n.d.). Quotes about humility. Retrieved from http://www.goodreads.com/quotes/tag/humility

Jennings, G. (2016, May 25). The rule of three. [Blog post]. Retrieved from http://www.museumcommons.com/2016/05/the-rule-of-three.html

Kadoyama, M. (2007, July). The spot where it flows: Practicing civic engagement (American Association of Museums Web Exclusive). Retrieved from http://margaretkadoyama.com/files123/Spot_Where_it_Flows.pdf

Kadoyama M. (2015, September 3). Program perspectives: True listening. [Western Museums Association blog post]. Retrieved from http://www.westmuse.org/articles/program-perspectives-true-listening

Le, Vu. (2016, September 6). 9 traits of the kind of leaders we need in this time and place. [Blog post]. Retrieved from http://nonprofitwithballs.com/2016/09/9-traits-of-the-kind-of-leaders-we-need-in-this-time-and-place/

Lewis, E. (2016, May). *Diversity: From talk to action*. Session conducted at the annual meeting of the American Alliance of Museums, Washington, DC.

Lindahl, K. (n.d.). Principles of dialogue. Retrieved from http://www.uri.org/files/resource_files/Principles%20of%20Dialogue%20by%20Kay%20Lindahl.pdf

Mandela, N. (2010). *Conversations with myself*. New York: Picador.

Museum Hue. (n.d.). Retrieved from https://www.facebook.com/Museumhue/

Museum Workers Speak. (n.d.) Retrieved from http://museumworkersspeak.weebly.com/

Museums Association. (2016). *Valuing diversity: The case for inclusive museums*. [Report by Jessica Turtle]. London. Retrieved from http://www.museumsassociation.org/download?id=1194934

Palmer, P. (2015, May 20). *Parker Palmer commencement address "Living from the inside out."* [Video file]. Retrieved from https://www.youtube.com/watch?v=MaOFkumhcCU

Racial Equity Tools. (n.d.). Retrieved from https://www.racialequitytools.org/home

Ramsey, F. [chescaleigh]. (2014, November 22). *5 Tips for being an ally*. [Video file]. Retrieved from https://www.youtube.com/watch?v=_dg86g-QlM0

Restorative Justice for Oakland Youth. (n.d.). Restorative justice. Retrieved from http://rjoyoakland.org/restorative-justice/

Rinpoche, S. M. (2015, March 16). True listening. Retrieved from http://shambhalatimes.org/2015/03/16/true-listening-2/

San Francisco Public Library. (n.d.). Exhibitions & programs. Retrieved from https://sfpl.org/index.php?pg=2000028701

Satterwhite, F., Teng, S., & Fernandopulle, A. (2007, July). *Cultural competency in capacity building*. Organizational Development & Capacity in Cultural Competence: Building Knowledge and Practice monograph series. CompassPoint Nonprofit Services. Retrieved from https://www.compasspoint.org/sites/default/files/documents/Satterwhite_full.pdf

Smith Kliebe, L. (Ed.). (2010). *Sing me your story, dance me home: Art and poetry from Native California – The Community Connections Project: Perspectives & tools for museum professionals.* California Exhibition Resources Alliance [now Exhibit Envoy]. Retrieved from http://www.exhibitenvoy.org/Portals/0/Exhibits/SMS/CERA%20SMS%20Tool%20Kit%20FINAL.pdf

The Incluseum. (n.d.). Retrieved from https://incluseum.com/

Thiederman, S. (2014). Engaged listening versus eloquent talking. Retrieved from http://thiederman.com/engaged-listening-versus-eloquent-talking/

Transforming Violence. (n.d.). Eloquent listening. Retrieved from http://www.transformingviolence.org/3_communityevents.html#eloquent

University of Kansas Work Group for Community Health and Development Community Tool Box. (n.d.). Section 7. Building Culturally Competent Organizations. Retrieved from http://ctb.ku.edu/en/table-of-contents/culture/cultural-competence/culturally-competent-organizations/main

University of Wisconsin Office of Equity, Diversity and Inclusion. (2015, March). Writing an effective position description. Retrieved from https://inclusion.uwex.uwc.edu/sites/inclusion.uwex.uwc.edu/files/writing_an_effective_position_description.pdf

Visitors of Color. (n.d.). Retrieved from http://visitorsofcolor.tumblr.com/

Wing Luke Museum of the Asian Pacific American Experience. (n.d.). At The Wing. Retrieved from http://www.wingluke.org/at-wing

Wing Luke Museum of the Asian Pacific American Experience. (n.d.). Community process. Retrieved from http://www.wingluke.org/community-process

Wing Luke Museum of the Asian Pacific American Experience. (n.d.). Go beyond our walls. Retrieved from http://www.wingluke.org/go-beyond-our-walls-1

Wing Luke Museum of the Asian Pacific American Experience. (n.d.). Our process. Retrieved from http://www.wingluke.org/our-process

Wing Luke Museum of the Asian Pacific American Experience. (n.d.). Our values. Retrieved from http://www.wingluke.org/our-values-1

7

LEARNING ABOUT COMMUNITIES AND CREATING A COMMUNITY PROFILE

How does one become a practitioner of community involvement? Often, it is a good idea to start small, learning along the way. The first step is considering *why* it is important to involve community members in the museum and *why* it is important for the museum to be involved in its community.

The "Why"

Consider the mission and vision of the museum as well as the museum's overall goals and aspirations. When museums build lasting relationships with the community, new bonds are formed, new audiences are identified and served, and the museum's network widens. Every community has its own community organizers and leaders, and there are often strong networks established among those who practice community activism. If the commitment to community-based work is apparent, museums are welcomed into this network. When museums forge these bonds, they develop relationships with community leaders, who then become advocates for the museum in the broader community. Sometimes, as their involvement with the museum deepens they become potential candidates for the museum's board, advisory committees, and staff. They also become part of the museum's network to identify candidates for open positions and potential volunteers.

The "How"

At first, the process of community involvement is internally focused, as leadership and staff learn about their organization and learn about themselves. The next step is considering and articulating *why* it is important to be involved with one's community. Now, the task is to consider *how* staff members learn about their communities and what types of research will illuminate community interests, assets, and concerns.

How might this information be used? What are the opportunities and challenges that might arise as museum staff members begin learning about communities?

The research process considers the context of the community and the museum locally, regionally, and nationally. The process describes how to begin learning about communities, how to embrace what one learns, and how to incorporate community learning and community involvement into everyday museum practice. It takes *investment* of time, resources, and personnel. It takes *commitment*. For research and evaluation to be effective, one must see it through and be willing to take action.

An early step in learning about communities is to consider the communities the museum leadership and staff want to learn about. The following questions and guidelines will be useful during this process.

Overall Guidelines for Determining Priority Communities

As museum leadership and staff begin to identify the priority communities they want to connect with more fully, they will want to be intentional and consider *why* they are interested in a specific community. Consider the following:

- The more *specific* the leadership and staff can be in identifying the priority communities, the better their research will be.
- Adding specific geographic parameters, such as neighborhoods, towns, or cities, is helpful in defining the community. When the Oakland Museum of California identified the four ZIP codes adjacent to the museum as its priority neighborhoods, it recognized the importance of this hyperlocal community. This helps the organization focus more precisely on who it wants to connect with and why. It provides at least some initial boundaries on where to begin the research. Those boundaries or parameters may shift over time or they may be expanded, but they are very helpful in the initial stages of this research.
- Is it a community? Think about ways that community members come together. Some groupings are demographically defined – for example, seniors in San Francisco or young adults in Minneapolis. This does not make it a community. However, if staff members are interested in connecting more fully with groups such as these, they might say that the priority community is the group of people who live in retirement homes/senior housing in specific neighborhoods in San Francisco, such as Japantown, Lower Pacific Heights, or the Mission District. Considering the ways that people come together will help in connecting and building relationships with the community groups. It helps to recognize that "community" is not the same as "audience." In community involvement, we are talking about communities.

Key Questions to Consider in Determining Priority Communities

A key process in determining the priority communities calls for the museum leadership and staff to consider several *strategic* questions, noted below. When these questions are addressed at the beginning of a community involvement initiative, they generate organization-wide discussions about community involvement, and staff members are able to see more clearly how community involvement is (or can be) a part of what they already do – that it can be a regular part of the organization's operations. When the museum leadership and staff see community involvement and learning about specific communities as an integral part of the museum's operations and programming, they will understand that asking these questions is part of their day-to-day process. Answering the following key questions will guide the leadership and staff to be strategic in determining priority communities:

- What is on the horizon for the museum in the next one to two years? What are the museum's plans? Working with priority communities that align with what the museum is already doing is a good place to start. Is there an exhibition, set of programs, or other initiative that the museum is already planning that will be a natural fit?

- How does this initiative align with/address the museum's strategic plan? To be most effective and sustainable, a clear alignment with the museum's strategic plan and institutional vision is necessary. An example of how involving a specific community in significant ways is at the core of a small museum's vision is provided later in this chapter. Aligning a community involvement initiative with the museum's strategic plan helps to embed the community involvement plan's goals and strategies in the organization's overall operations rather than making it an add-on.

- What information do the staff members already have about specific communities? What do they know about the specific areas? Are the neighborhoods residential? Are they mixed business/residential? What are the demographics of the residents of this area (i.e., average age, household income, number of households with children under 18, race and ethnicity, other demographic data)? Making an informed decision about priority communities is based, in part, on what information museum leadership and staff already have about a specific community. Some baseline answers to these questions can be found through the national census. Considering what information staff and leadership already have about an area will help them understand what they need to find out.

- What do the leadership and staff already know about the museum's *current* audiences? The work that was done for the institutional assessment will help a great deal at this point, including information about past program partners. Look particularly at the answers to questions about outreach and specific audiences, such as those focusing on past efforts to engage with specific audiences, whether they have been sustained, and what the staff may have learned from the experience. Look at other community partnership projects the museum has done and why it engaged in these partnerships, whether the projects have continued, and whether museum leadership and staff continue to keep in touch with the organizations and people even if the specific project ended. The answers to these questions about specific audiences and partnership projects will help the museum leadership and staff to understand more about how they approach this work and what they might need to consider going forward.

- Are the leadership and staff ready to create a list of potential priority communities, including a paragraph or description about *why* each is a priority community? This may come from the museum's mission and vision statements, strategic plan, or other documents. As the leadership and staff consider potential communities to focus on, why are they interested in those particular communities? Specific answers to these questions will guide the museum as it narrows its focus on priority communities. For instance, is this a close-by neighborhood? Perhaps the museum staff knows from previous audience research that local residents are not coming to the museum, and the staff would like to know why so they can address those constraints and be involved in their immediate community. Perhaps the museum leadership and staff are re-interpreting and re-installing some of the permanent exhibits and want to highlight new stories and new communities and more fully involve the communities in telling the stories.

  When museum leadership and staff go out into the community to learn about the people, businesses, and organizations that make up this community, they will want to speak knowledgeably about *why* the museum is interested in connecting with that community and serving community members more fully.

- What, specifically, do the museum leadership and staff want to know about the community, and how will they use this information? Articulating what someone wants to know and how they will use this information guides the research process. The Learning About the Community: Suggested Methods section later in this chapter provides additional guidance.

- Do the museum leadership and staff already know people who are associated with this community? This is a critical question to address, especially when considering priority communities. When museum leadership and staff have existing connections with community stakeholders, people who live and/or work in that community, they have access to perspectives that will inform their research. When staff members first begin learning about a community, it helps a great deal if their friends, supporters, and colleagues can provide introductions or the names of people they know in this community. Are there people, organizations, or websites that the leadership and staff know about that can help the staff learn about the focus communities? Asking all staff, volunteers, and board members whether they know anyone or have connections with any person or organization in the priority communities could result in potential resources. If they can provide introductions to people or contact information and the names of people to interview, this would be very helpful. The staff will need to launch into their research about the community, and any way that the museum leadership, staff, and volunteers can smooth the way will help them.

Answering these key questions will guide the leadership and staff to be strategic in determining the priority communities. When done thoughtfully and strategically, this process will enable a deeper level of community involvement.

Articulating the Value of the Museum in the Community

Museum leadership and staff need to have a clear idea of the *value* that museums bring to building healthy communities. These values might include providing educational resources for community groups, providing expertise in specific areas, and serving as a linkage between the community and influential business and political leaders. Museum leadership and staff can identify what the museum brings to the process of building healthier communities through asking the entire staff to identify the skills and resources they have. In addition, a mini-visitor survey can elicit visitors' comments about what they think the museum brings to a community. In their opinion, what is the value of the museum? Compile this information and share it with everyone in the organization so that everyone realizes the assets and resources the museum has. Internal and external research will reveal a number of attributes that are of value in community work. Staff will learn a great deal about the organization and what it brings to the community. This new perspective can crystallize into a vision of the museum as being an integral part of building a healthy community.

Creating a Community Profile

After the museum leadership and staff have completed the internal assessment and identified appropriate communities with whom they want to connect more fully, it is time to focus on learning about the priority communities. Staff can use a number of ways to do this, including conducting quantitative and qualitative research. When organizations involve many staff members in this research process, they benefit by learning more about the communities and by beginning to form more connections with community members. Each staff person who is actively engaged in this can embrace the effort and support it, thereby increasing the number of internal champions.

As staff members begin to learn about the community and begin to create a community profile, consider who will receive the community profile report. Will it be shared with the full leadership and staff? Will it be shared with advisory committees? When the researchers write the report, they will want to keep the priority audiences in mind, as this will guide the tone of the report and what level of detail is needed. For example, the staff who focus on exhibition development, programming, fundraising and grants, and marketing may all need specific information about the interests, concerns, and assets as well as the names and contact information of community stakeholders.

Consider whether the information will be shared with others outside the organization. Will the museum leadership and staff share what they learned with community members? This is an important aspect of community work, and it requires intentional planning. Community members' past experience may be that other organizations have come into their community to do research and left without giving back to the community – without sharing the results of what they learned. Community members may feel that your museum is one more group coming into their community to do research – to take from them and not give back. Intentional planning about how to share the information with community members will help to build trust.

When an organization is in the process of learning about a community and is preparing the information for distribution, the leadership and staff will need to talk with community members to learn how they would like to be included, what format they would like to receive information, and how the research might be useful for community members. This will help to pave the way for continuing and nurturing the relationships that are being developed.

The community profile may be presented in any number of formats (written report, slide presentations, etc.). The intent is to gather all that the museum is learning about the priority community and describe the characteristics of the community it is learning about.

As leadership and staff create the community profile, consider the following guiding questions. The clearer the museum is in its answers, the clearer the community profile will be.

1. Who are the people who make up this community, and where do they live?

   - The first part of this question is purposely vague, but it gives museum staff members a chance to begin by writing everything they know about this community. If staff or leadership know any individuals who are part of this community, indicate that here. This is also where museum staff members will write everything they *think* they know about this community. As the research progresses and the museum leadership and staff gather data and learn about the people who make up the community and where they live, their preliminary answers to this question will be adjusted and refined. Initial assumptions will be challenged, and the data that is gathered by the staff will be useful in answering this question more completely.

   - The second part of this question is where the museum can consider the geographic parameters of where community members live. The national census (see Demographic Research below) may have relevant information that is very accessible and useful.

2. What are the primary institutions and organizations that support this community?

   - Think about the ways the leadership and staff defined the priority community, and look to the criteria within that definition to help guide the research for this question. For example, if the priority community is "families from a specific neighborhood in our city," perhaps the primary institutions and organizations that support this community would be local schools, Boys and Girls Clubs, YMCAs, local sports clubs, family service agencies, and local community centers. Each of these organizations has valuable perspectives about the community, and collectively they can provide insights that help museum staff get to know and understand the community. During the initial research, it is useful to identify a number of organizations that potentially might be primary organizations in this community. More extensive research into each organization and institution will reveal which are primary organizations and which are not as relevant for the priority community.

3. Who are the community leaders and stakeholders?

   • Stakeholders are often people who have a strong interest in creating a healthier community. They may be the staff members who work at the primary institutions and organizations that support the community (see above). They may be neighborhood watch captains, people who have owned businesses in the neighborhood for a long time, and city council members. How to identify potential key stakeholders is explored in the next section.

4. What are the primary concerns, interests, and needs of this community?

   • This is at the heart of the research – where the leadership and staff will learn what is on community members' minds. The other questions in this section help to prepare the museum leadership and staff to focus on this key question. See the next section for guidance in ways to learn about this.

5. What assets exist within this community?

   • As discussed in Chapter 1, this book uses an asset-based model when considering communities. Communities already have assets and capacities that are useful in addressing community concerns. People in communities already have great stores of knowledge and understanding, and it is leadership's and staff's responsibility to learn about these. When considering capacities and assets, it will be useful to identify all the ways that assets may exist in a community. Human assets, such as the community leaders and stakeholders, are often the first ones whom museum staff and leadership will encounter. What are the skills, talents, and capacities of the human assets – the people who live and work in a community? These might range from organizing skills (e.g., block captains) to caretaking (e.g., day care and eldercare). These skills are assets and are particularly valuable when community planning and action groups form. Consider that when community planning and action groups meet, will childcare and/or eldercare be provided? This is one example of how individual assets within a community are valuable. Similarly, what are the capacities of the organizations and informal associations in the community? A recognition and examination of the skills, talents, and capacities of organizations and informal associations will reveal assets that are important tools in building healthier communities.

6. What are the primary complexities and nuances of this community – things that the museum leadership and staff would need to know to build a sustainable relationship with this community?

   • Addressing this question focuses on *assessing what someone is learning as they learn*. Chapter 1 discussed how communities are complex. At times someone may be tempted to describe communities in simplistic ways, but sometimes communities are divided entities. Even within a small community, there are many perspectives, and it is important to recognize that there may be significant differences of opinions. Within a single community, there may be people who are affluent, not so affluent, old, young, and in between. A community may well encompass different ethnic groups with different – and sometimes conflicting – histories. These are the complexities and nuances to pay attention to.

7. What is the economic profile of this community?

   • This question is included so that someone can use the data from the national census to get an overall perspective of the economic resources available in a community. It supplements much of the other information that is gathered, presenting an image of the community as a whole.

8. What businesses and community centers are primary to this community?

   • This is similar to question 2, but it also prompts the researcher to look at businesses in the community. Businesses, and the people who work in them, are part of a community's resources and assets.

9. Where do community members learn about community programs, events, and meetings that are important in the community?

   • Considering where community members learn about community meetings and events gives staff members a good indication of where they will need to be to be part of the communication network and what they will need to do.

10. How much do community members use online sources to communicate with one another, and how much do they use online sources to learn about what's happening in the community?

   • This is related to question 9, but more specifically about online communication, including social media. This may also vary within a community, especially when one considers different generations' use of online resources and social media.

11. What barriers or constraints exist that prevent or hinder this community from fuller involvement with one's museum?

   • This is also at the heart of a museum's research, a corollary to question 4. Assessing the barriers and constraints so that staff can address them is core to effective community involvement. These barriers and constraints may be physical (e.g., how accessible is the museum? How convenient is it to get there via public transportation? Is sufficient free parking available? Is the museum open during evenings and weekends?). They may be psychological (e.g., how welcome do I feel here? Do I see people like me? Is there anything here that is important to me?). They may be economic (e.g., the cost for my family to go to the museum is too high when we take into consideration transportation/parking, admission tickets for all of us, and food. We would rather spend that money elsewhere). Identifying and understanding the barriers and constraints that hinder fuller community involvement will help museum staff and leadership to address them.

12. How has leadership in this community changed? Are there younger leaders emerging?

- Considering this question helps build awareness of additional complexities within communities. Perhaps the voices of people who have been community leaders for many years are now being joined by the voices of younger people. Pay attention to who is quoted, whom one hears about, and whose voices are more evident. Being aware of who is and is not included helps staff to understand the complexity.

13. What materials, archives, photographs, records, etc. do community members have that might be of interest to a museum?

- Community members may not consider that their materials are important enough for a museum to collect. They may feel that the letters, photos, and archives are of personal interest but not of interest to anyone else. As someone is learning about the community and they develop relationships with community members, they will want to be aware of this and invite conversations to find out more.

14. What are the leisure-time activities of this community?

- Understanding how community members spend free-choice time is crucial to understanding the components that impact their decisions about museumgoing. What is important to them in their free-choice time? How much time do community members have each week to spend on leisure activities? The answers to these questions will help museum staff understand how community members want to spend their limited leisure time. It might also lead to the museum leadership and staff considering new ideas for partnership projects. For instance, if community members spend their free-choice time participating in family activities (a picnic in a park on a Sunday, for example), museum staff members and leadership may consider partnering with local community centers to offer park-based activities for different ages.

15. How much importance do community members place on cultural organizations like museums?

- Related to question 14, this helps staff understand how much value community members place on cultural organizations and whether they want to spend their free-choice time there. It can also lead to more nuanced questions. For instance, will partnering with other types of organizations (in other sectors) connect museums with community members who don't place a high value on cultural organizations?

16. How much importance do community members place on the subject matter of one's museum?

- Also related to questions 14 and 15, this question focuses on content rather than experience.

17. Do community members visit museums in general and one's museum in particular?

- What are community members' experiences with the organization? A more detailed review of past visitor studies at the museum may reveal new insights.

As leadership and staff address these questions during their research, various research methods are useful and are included below. The research will enable staff to create a community profile and description, which should give a clear idea of the *character* of the community and its primary concerns and interests.

Learning About the Community: Suggested Methods

As the museum leadership and staff begin to learn about the community and consider the questions above, a variety of methods will help them gain deeper understanding about the community. These methods include demographic research, online research, on-site fieldwork, interviews with key informants, and community conversations. To determine which methods to use and when to use them, the museum leadership and staff engage in preliminary planning to address the following:

- **Articulating** what the leadership and staff want to find out: What do the museum leadership and staff want to know about the community? What will they do with the information – how will they use what they learn? The more completely they answer these questions, the more effective their research will be. The answers to these questions should align with the earlier work the museum leadership and staff did when they described their intentions about engaging in a museum–community involvement initiative (see Chapter 6).
- **Identifying** what kinds of information staff needs to gather: Will the staff need to collect quantitative information, qualitative information, or both? Which methods will provide this information? To learn about the community, the museum's leadership and staff will most likely need to use both quantitative and qualitative methods. The following sections provide more detail about the uses

of each type of information and some helpful guidelines in determining which research methods will be most useful for obtaining each type. Since so much of the focus is on developing relationships with community members, this book emphasizes qualitative methods as a way to connect person to person.

- **Identifying** specific considerations: What challenges might staff members encounter as they learn about the specific community?

  o   For example, might community members be hesitant to share their perspectives with people they don't know? How will the museum leadership and staff get to know community members and begin to build trust so that these concerns are addressed? How will the leadership and staff become culturally competent so that they approach this process of learning with respect and humility?

  o   What do museum leadership and staff already know about this community? Soliciting and gathering this information from internal sources will provide an initial picture of the community.

  o   What assumptions do leadership and staff have? In Chapter 6, paying attention to and articulating one's assumptions was described as a way to learn about oneself. It also helps people plan effective research strategies. When staff and leadership are in the process of learning about a community, acknowledging their assumptions helps to develop research strategies that diminish the biases that these assumptions may bring to the study. As an example, perhaps the staff members are interested in learning more about the people who are residents of senior communities in their town so they can work more closely with them to provide services. What assumptions are staff members making about the seniors? Are there nuances about cultural groups that they need to know?

  o   What resources are available to learn about this community? This may include websites, blogs, organizations, community stakeholders and leaders, publications, community bulletin boards, and many other sources.

- **Creating a plan** to gather the information: What specific questions will staff members ask? Who will they ask? Who will provide the perspective staff members need to answer the museum's primary questions? In creating a plan to gather the information, museum leadership and staff develop a process to address the questions they have asked. The following sections provide guidance in creating this plan.

- **Gathering** and recording the information: Suggested information to collect and forms to share this information among staff are described later in this chapter, and sample forms are included in Appendix A (Community Research Update Form, Online Research Form, and Community Involvement Master Contact List).

- **Analyzing** the information and creating a plan that utilizes what museum leadership and staff learn. Chapter 8 focuses on creating a plan.

BOX 7.1 KEY QUESTIONS FOR LEARNING ABOUT THE COMMUNITY

- What do you want to know?
- What questions do you want to answer?
- What kind of information will you need to gather to answer those questions?
- Will you need to collect quantitative information, qualitative information, or both?
- Which methods will provide this information?
- What challenges might you encounter as you learn about the community?
- What do you already know about the community?
- What assumptions do you have?
- What resources are available to learn about this community?
- What specific questions will you ask?
- Whom will you ask? Who will provide the perspective you need to answer your primary questions?

The following are brief descriptions of useful methods to learn about communities.

Quantitative: Demographic Research

Demographic research provides a set of data that numerically describes a community. The national census is a primary source for useful information. For example, in the United States, the U.S. Census describes geographic communities in terms of specific criteria, as defined by the U.S. government. They include statistics about race, gender, ethnicity, household type, income, and family type. The American FactFinder section of the U.S. Census website provides data about selected economic characteristics, such as employment status; types of occupation; industries represented; income; and business statistics, such as number of businesses and number of employees. Demographic data is a small but important part of the full picture of one's community, and it is important to include this data in the community profile. It supplements the information gathered through online research and community consultation. There are a number of additional sources for demographic data beyond the census, and they include local and regional planning departments, universities, and state-specific data from state departments of education and state departments of finance.

Online Research

A great deal of information is available online, from websites of local organizations to community newsletters to online communities. Doing a web search on any aspect of the community will likely yield numerous sites. It is important to keep in mind what the researcher is looking for so they don't get sidetracked on sites that don't provide relevant information or perspectives.

Consider what types of sites might be useful, and start with those. As staff members begin to research, they will need to remember to:

- Keep track of what types of information they find, where they find it, and how useful it may be. See Appendix A, Community Research Update Form and Online Research Form, for examples of ways to keep track of information.
- Pay attention to who is active in the community, who is quoted, who journalists interview, etc. These are often the community stakeholders, and their perspectives are helpful in gaining a more complete understanding about the community.
- Think about what types of organizations, individuals, businesses, and/or agencies might have information about this community. How might staff access them? These could include:
  o City websites;
  o Chambers of commerce;
  o City's convention and visitors bureau;
  o The state-wide visitors bureau;
  o MediaPost publications (online publications and blog posts focused on specific areas, including marketing information to engage various groups, such as Hispanics, kids 6–11, moms, Gen Y, and boomers);
  o Neighborhood-specific sites, such as NextDoor (serve as online bulletin boards about neighborhood-specific concerns).

Surveys

Surveys are an effective way to learn specific types of information and are most useful if a researcher wants to hear from many people. There are a variety of online survey sites that provide tools and platforms to conduct surveys. As part of gathering data, staff members may determine that they would like to hear from a number of people, they have a few specific questions to ask, and they have access to groups of people who would be willing to provide their opinions and perspectives. Perhaps staff members are interested in engaging with the students at their local community college, and they would like to learn more about how the students spend their time when they are not in class or working. Or staff members are interested in knowing more about how teachers utilize the museum's resources. They might create an online survey, set up a table in an accessible location where their priority audience is physically present, and ask people to answer a few survey questions using a mobile device, such as a tablet. A web search on surveys will yield links to various tools and platforms that will allow staff members to conduct surveys for free or low cost. A simple online survey is a good way to get started and enables a researcher to see what types of information are available.

Qualitative Research: Interviews and Community Conversations

Qualitative research – through interviews, community conversations, and focus groups – can be a very useful way to learn about communities. Interviews are an extended form of conversation, one that is guided and allows for probing for deeper content. Interviews provide an opportunity to begin the process of building deeper relationships with community members. When staff members go through the process of articulating what they want to find out and they determine that they want to collect qualitative information, they begin by identifying key stakeholders, people whose perspectives are important to understanding the community, as potential interviewees. Interviews are a way to connect with people who are trusted in the community, who can help staff learn about the community and open doors for staff members to connect with community members.

How do staff members identify key stakeholders whose perspectives will help them understand more about the community? Start with looking internally at who museum leadership and staff already know and doing online research. In addition, fieldwork is important. If staff members are learning about a geographic community, go to the area in person and spend time in the neighborhood. Go into one or two businesses or community centers in the area, and note which businesses are there. Are there restaurants or corner markets? Go in and make a purchase, and consider what it might be like to live in that neighborhood. What community organizations serve the community? Observe and pay attention. Key stakeholders are located in all these places. As Paul Mattessich and Barbara Monsey note in *Community Building: What Makes It Work*,

> Successful [community building] efforts more likely occur in communities with existing, identifiable leadership. That is, they tend to occur in communities containing at least some residents who most community members will follow and listen to, who can motivate and act as spokespersons, and who can assume leadership roles in a community building initiative.

Mattessich and Monsey go on to ask these questions:

- Does the community have members who are already taking on visible leadership positions (scout leaders, religious leaders, people who organize community events)? Are these people available and interested in doing additional community building?
- Does the community have a reservoir of leadership, as yet overlooked, in the form of leaders such as Head Start parents or block-watchers?

Mattessich and Monsey, 1997, pp. 25, 26

At times, community stakeholders are referred to as *community gatekeepers*, and this is sometimes used to identify individuals (stakeholders) who, to some degree, control access into a community. This may be formal access, when one needs to have official approval to proceed with a project, or informal, when one needs to connect with community members and they find that there is skepticism about the project and one's motives. When staff members begin to learn about their priority communities, they will want to keep an eye and ear open to whether there are gatekeepers in the communities. There are many kinds of community gatekeepers. Some may take it upon themselves to control access to communities (and not necessarily because other community members have granted them this authority), and some may be given this authority because they are trusted by other community members.

It will be important to create and nurture trusting relationships with a number of community members and gatekeepers from the very beginning of the process. When one is learning about one's communities, and in conversations with community members, pay attention to whom they mention as people they listen to and whom they suggest talking to.

Museum staff and leadership can learn more about a community by attending neighborhood association meetings, meetings of the town council and/or planning commission, volunteer organizations, and other community gatherings that are open to the public. Go to the markets, churches, and other places where people gather. Pay attention. Look for opportunities to connect with others who are focused on building healthier communities. Specific opportunities to meet people, learn about the community, and begin to build relationships include:

- *Neighborhood associations*: In many cases, people form neighborhood associations to work on specific neighborhood concerns. As a member of a specific neighborhood, it is essential that the museum be represented in the neighborhood association. The museum representative(s) will be a voice at the table, offering the museum's resources to assist in furthering the neighborhood association's goals, advocating for the museum, and expressing the museum's desire and commitment to being a good neighbor. Neighborhood associations may include residents, merchants, law enforcement and other city services, the faith community, and community service organizations. To find out whether a neighborhood association exists in the museum's community, contact local residents and businesses. Read the local newspapers, noting who is involved in local activities, and ask at the city council/board of supervisors. Find out when the group meets, and go to the meetings. It is likely that museum staff and leadership will be welcomed.

- *Merchant associations/chambers of commerce*: The museum is a part of the business community, and every aspect of that community is of concern to the museum. Merchant associations and chambers of commerce advocate on behalf of the business community, and they are good opportunities to meet and get to know local business leaders. They are engaged in many initiatives and projects to create healthier communities, including neighborhood cleanup and beautifying projects and partnership activities with local nonprofits.

- *Service organizations*: Leadership and staff will find many opportunities for working together with community members on community service projects.

Working together is a very effective way to get to know others in one's community and to begin building relationships. There are numerous service clubs, including Rotary International, Optimist International, Kiwanis, Soroptomist International, and many others. Check the Internet under *Community Service and Volunteerism: Organizations* and find out which ones are most active in the area.

• *Consortiums of organizations and individuals who come together for a specific purpose*: Consortiums are often very effective ways to network with a variety of people, and they are formed to address very specific issues. For instance, in San Francisco several years ago, an initiative to build healthier communities was established. Called "Neighborhoods in Transition: A Multicultural Partnership," it was a coalition of many different people and organizations, centered in nine different neighborhoods throughout the city, with the purpose of addressing economic and social concerns.

Another example is the Marin Human Rights Roundtable on the Prevention of Hate Violence, a consortium of thirty-five community organizations working to prevent hate violence in Marin County, California. The roundtable included representatives from ethnically specific groups, the faith community, law enforcement, the human rights commission, fair housing advocates, gay/lesbian/bisexual/ transgender groups, and many others. All the organizations that were part of the roundtable focused on building healthier communities, and the consortium provided an excellent way for these organizations to build trusting relationships.

Consortiums like these exist formally and informally in many places, and museum representatives are welcomed in the coalitions.

The diagram below (Figure 7.1) from *Building Communities from the Inside Out* illustrates the ways in which local community organizations can work together to build healthier communities – in this case using a local park as a way to rebuild a community (Kretzmann & McKnight, 1993, p. 187).

Early Steps in Connecting with Key Stakeholders

As museum staff and leadership identify key stakeholders whose perspectives will help them understand more about the community, they can also consider the *internal* stakeholders – staff, board, volunteers, and docents – to help them understand more about who internal stakeholders know.

The actions to connect with key stakeholders include:

• Create a list of potential interviewees or focus group members. Staff members have done a good deal of research and identified a number of individuals whose perspectives will help the museum leadership and staff understand more about the community. Think about which of these stakeholders the museum would like to connect with first. Are there any stakeholders that the leadership, staff, and volunteers already know? It helps a great deal when someone who is trusted

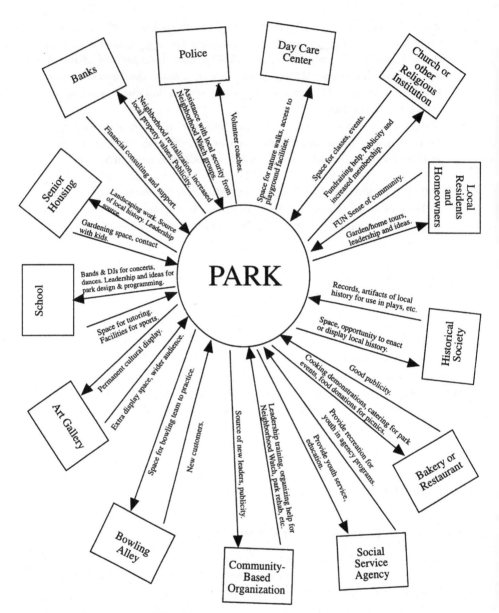

FIGURE 7.1 One-on-one relationships.

Courtesy of ABCD Institute.

in the community – someone community members already know – can provide an introduction and open the door. Perhaps staff members have already connected with someone at a community meeting, someone whose perspectives the museum wants to hear. Add the names to the list of stakeholders who may be potential interviewees.

- Prioritize the list of potential interviewees and determine who will follow up with each person. When the museum involves more people in the organization in the work of learning about and connecting with community members, it will have more points of connection – a way to create a full network. Including staff, volunteers, and board members builds support internally and externally. If someone internally suggested the name or knows the person, it would be advantageous for them to be the one to follow up with that person to begin developing the relationship. Later, the staff member can introduce the person to others at the museum and begin to widen the network.

- Spend time in the neighborhood. Note what businesses are there and what community organizations serve the community. There may be key stakeholders and potential interviewees that one finds through spending time there.

- Set up the initial interviews. Begin by calling the potential interviewee, following up with an immediate email. Leave a message if the person is not available. Have a short introduction to explain what the call is about. For example, a follow-up email might say:

"I'm following up on a phone message I just left for you. [*Your mutual friend*] suggested I contact you for some help with a project for [*your*] museum. I am working with [*your museum*], and we would like to connect more closely with [*your community*] to make sure that what we do is relevant to the community and addresses community interests and concerns. Part of this process involves talking with community people, and [*your mutual friend*] highly recommended that I talk with you. Your perspective would be invaluable in this process!

"I'll be conducting short interviews during the next couple of weeks, and I would very much appreciate it if you would agree to be interviewed/ answer a few questions for this. The interview should take about twenty minutes. Would you have time to provide your insights? If so, what are some good days and times for me to meet with (or call) you?"

See Appendix A for sample email letters.

- Be polite; let the person know that their perspective is valued and that your mutual friend suggested that you talk with them.

- If you are successful in contacting the person, make an appointment for the interview. In-person interviews are most effective for beginning to establish a relationship, but they are more time-consuming than phone interviews. Phone interviews are efficient and useful ways to get information, but they are not as effective as in-person interviews in allowing the unexpected conversation path to emerge. Email interviews, where the researcher sends written questions to the interviewee and the interviewee sends written responses, are useful in getting information but are not as effective in building a relationship.

- Send written confirmation of your appointment. You might also offer to send the list of questions ahead of time.
- Create the questions. Create a set of interview questions that addresses what staff and leadership want to know.

  o Be clear on what staff and leadership want to know and how they will use the information. For any question, add in "so that ...". For example, a researcher might say "I want to know where people in this community spend their off-work time so that I can make sure I include that location/community center/other space in my work." "We want to know more about the organizations that work closely with this community so that we can get to know the people who work there and possibly engage in partnerships with them."

  o Formulate questions to produce in-depth responses, not yes or no. Test questions for effectiveness by doing a few practice interviews with fellow staff members. Pay attention to how each question sounds to the listener. Is it clear? Does it elicit complete and rich responses? If not, the questions need to be fine-tuned until they are clear.

  o Questions should be sensitive. Ask colleagues, especially those who have a different perspective, to review the questions and suggest sensitive and respectful ways of asking. This does not mean that the initial question is insensitive or disrespectful. People have implicit biases that they often are not aware of. Asking people with different perspectives to review the questions results in thoughtful questions that reflect a broader perspective. When asking colleagues for this input, offer to reciprocate.

  o Limit the interview to twenty minutes, but go longer if it's working well or shorter if needed. If the staff members are having challenges securing interviews, they may consider choosing three questions that are particularly important and asking people to spend about five to ten minutes in a conversation. They are focusing on *learning* about the community. This is not a formal research project, so being flexible with the interview protocol is fine.

  o Prepare seven to ten questions, and be ready to ask additional questions to learn more (e.g., "Can you tell me more about that?").

Things to Consider When Developing Interview Questions

- Make questions accessible, using common words, not jargon. The practice interviews will help the interviewer know whether they are using jargon and where they may need to use more common terms.
- Prioritize the most essential questions. What does the staff really want to know from this interview? Focus on that. The order of the questions matters – the interviewer wants to establish a comfort level and trust with the interviewee.

So the first questions are more general, and the most essential (or more specific) questions follow those. See Appendix A for examples of interview questions. This is an interview protocol – a guideline – and the questions can be modified to elicit relevant responses.

- Think about the interview as a conversation. How will it flow? Organize the questions so they feel like they would be a good conversation.
- Start with a set of predetermined interview questions. However, be flexible enough to modify some questions based on the circumstances of a particular interview.
- Use basic good manners. Listen.
- Be persistent in the efforts to connect with people. It may take multiple attempts to contact people. Use the phone and email, and go to the community in person. Show up.
- Remember that community leaders are very busy and may not put a high priority on the museum's request for information.
- The community stakeholders whom the museum is contacting may well have answered similar questions from other researchers in the past. They may not be eager to respond to the museum staff's request, especially if they feel that researchers come into a community and take information and the community never benefits from the research. Be committed to getting back to community members and giving back.
- Remember to do the initial research – visit the organization's website and become familiar with it – and ask pertinent questions that allow the interviewee to share their unique perspective. Use their time wisely; don't ask questions that are already addressed on the organization's website.
- Practice, practice, practice – to become more comfortable with the process.
- Always thank the interviewee (and send a follow-up thank-you note) after they have taken the time to share their perspectives.
- Ask "Who else should I talk to?"
- If needed, revise the questions after initial interviews. Initial questions may not have been as clear as staff hoped. Revise the questions so they are clear.
- During the interviews, listen closely. When transcribing notes later, keep in mind that the people and organizations that staff are learning about may be potential partners for the museum. Were there any comments made by the interviewee that indicates they would welcome the opportunity to partner with the museum? Keep this in mind.
- Keep a record of staff's attempts to contact people. See Appendix A for a sample form, called Community Research Update Form.
- For students: If this is being done for a class project, keep the museum in mind. What does the museum need to know about the community to deepen the relationship between the museum and the community?
- For students: If this is being done for a class project, clarify to all potential interviewees that this is a class assignment, that you are working collaboratively with the museum but you are not on the museum staff. Let them know that

the report and recommendations are for suggestions only but that the museum is very interested in connecting and working with this community.

Stories from the Field: Key Stakeholders and Developing Relationships

The California Academy of Sciences (CAS or Academy) is a beloved institution. Bay Area children have grown up with it for generations. Established in 1853, it moved to Golden Gate Park in 1916 and continues to serve local, regional, national, and international audiences.

In 1989, the longtime executive director of the Japanese Community Youth Council (JCYC) in San Francisco contacted CAS leaders with an idea. He believed that the Academy would be a great venue for a family night for JCYC families, and he proposed such a program to Academy board and staff members. Academy staff worked closely with the JCYC leadership and staff to plan and host the family night at the Academy in the summer of 1989. Following this, the JCYC executive director worked closely with Academy staff to advocate for the Academy as a family-friendly venue and encouraged his peers, executive directors at San Francisco youth-serving community organizations, to partner with the Academy in family programs. In addition, a valued and trusting relationship was developing between Academy staff and the JCYC executive director and his staff. The two staffs worked with one another in collaborative programs, and JCYC staff assisted CAS staff by providing informal feedback on specific programs, publicizing events to the community, referring people for CAS staff positions, and doing other supportive, collaborative, and collegial actions. JCYC Family Nights were held in subsequent years, as well, and this relationship deepened.

After the Loma Prieta earthquake in October 1989, the Academy was included in a San Francisco bond measure to improve the seismic safety of several city-owned buildings. In the early months of 1990, the JCYC executive director called Academy staff and said, "I'd like to help support the Academy with getting this bond measure passed. What can I do?" This offer of support from a committed community leader was an unexpected benefit of an ongoing and deepening relationship with Academy staff and board members. The bond passed, with 78% of the vote, a testament to the support of the San Francisco community.

The CAS-JCYC story highlights one of the primary effects of deepening relationships between people and between organizations — that developing and deepening relationships can have unexpected outcomes. Museum leadership and staff may well have a plan for community involvement, but a plan is just part of the overall picture. Embracing museum–community involvement also means embracing the unknown and trusting that the deepening relationships are core to the museum's role in its community. There will often be discomfort in embracing the unknown; museum staff and leadership may fear what might happen when there is a deeper relationship with community organizations. Will the organizations ask to participate more in the museum's decisions? Will they push for their voices to be heard? Chapter 6 already highlighted some of the attributes that are critical for effective community involvement, including courage and the ability to address fears. When museum leadership and staff are fearful about the unknown, they can demonstrate courage by embracing the developing relationships with community members and organizations.

Another effect of deepening relationships is how they are, at their core, person-to-person connections. These person-to-person connections, when nurtured and expanded, can become person-to-organization and organization-to-organization relationships. These core person-to-person relationships can play out over years and involve various organizations. As leadership and staff move from initial partnership organizations into other community-based organizations, they bring these relationships with them, enabling new organizations to benefit from the trusting relationships developed and nurtured along the way.

Stories from the Field: Museum of Craft and Folk Art

The Museum of Craft and Folk Art (MOCFA) in San Francisco featured exhibitions and programs about traditional and contemporary folk art and craft. In 2002, MOCFA planned an exhibition about Native American glass, called *Fusing Traditions: Transformations in Glass by Native American Artists*. The museum's executive director was interested in working with a community advisory committee. The purpose of the community advisory committee was to be sensitive to the fact that the museum was crossing a significant cultural boundary with this exhibition and to have the cultural context present in the exhibit and program planning process and in the marketing plans.

The museum staff hoped that the advisory committee members would suggest and help plan public programs, events, and openings and help spread the word about the exhibition and programs. Museum staff wanted to honor the advisors' perspectives and ensure that the work would be equitable and not a burden on committee members. It was intended that the committee would meet three times over three months and carry on the rest of the work via email and phone.

The museum staff hoped that working with the community advisory committee would lead to lasting relationships with the committee members through getting to know individuals and stakeholders in the community. The staff also hoped that the advisors would become part of the museum's audience through continuing the relationship even after the exhibition closed.

The museum engaged a consultant to work with museum staff as they identified potential advisory committee members and created a list of people to invite to serve. The committee planned to include Native artists and scholars, Native community stakeholders, glass artists and scholars, and museum colleagues. The consultant called and emailed each potential advisor to begin developing a relationship and ascertain their interest in serving on this advisory committee. The consultant sent the following email, hoping it was warm and welcoming:

> I called because I'm working on a project that I thought might be of interest to you. The Museum of Craft and Folk Art (at Fort Mason Center)

is developing an exhibition and programs on contemporary glass art by Native American artists. The museum is putting together a community advisory committee of folks who are active in the Native American and glass communities who might be interested in giving suggestions for programs, reviewing label copy, and assisting in publicizing the exhibition. The museum staff is very interested in ensuring that the exhibition is culturally accessible and building relationships with community leaders. As we were suggesting people to be part of the committee, I thought of you and would consider it an honor if you would be part of this advisory committee. We will meet three times and do the rest of the work via email. Here's what we hope the community advisory committee members will do:

- Review label copy
- Assist in recommending programs to go along with the exhibition
- Publicize the exhibit and programs
- Encourage organizations to plan group visits to the exhibition
- Assist in recommending and/or recruiting docents
- Assist with providing the names of people and groups to contact to publicize the exhibition and programs

We will be meeting on Tuesday, March 26, from 6:00–7:30 p.m. at the museum, and I would love to have you be part of this committee. Sound interesting? I hope so!

I am attaching a brief description of the exhibition, so you can see why we're excited about this. Please let me know what you think. I hope you say yes!

As the MOCFA staff and consultant considered whose perspectives to include in the committee, they recognized the importance of connecting with the American Indian Studies Department in the College of Ethnic Studies at San Francisco State University (SFSU). SFSU's College of Ethnic Studies has been a leader – it was the first one established in the United States and continues to nurture and provide leadership. It made sense to connect with the American Indian Studies faculty when MOCFA, a San Francisco organization, began to create the advisory committee.

The consultant contacted the American Indian Studies Department chair to explore whether he would be interested in serving as an advisor. He recommended two faculty members, noting that they both would be great for this because of their work in the American Indian Studies Program at State and their knowledge of Native American art and music. The consultant contacted both of the suggested faculty, and they both said yes. They taught courses in American Indian art and music, and both are practicing artists.

The first advisory committee meeting was scheduled and held at the museum in the early evening. The staff welcomed people, thanked them for attending, and reiterated the value that their perspective would bring to the project. The first meeting included introductions, a description of the exhibit, orientation materials (including a list of staff contacts for specific areas), and a list of the committee members with contact information. The meeting also included a summary of the type of assistance that the staff was looking for: program ideas, publicity, press contacts, and planning group visits. As each staff person described their needs, the consultant encouraged people to think about how they could provide assistance and advice and to consider who else staff should talk to for follow-up suggestions. The committee members were mostly listening – this was the first time the group had met and was getting the full details about the exhibition. Some advisors knew one another already; others did not. Seven advisors participated in the first meeting along with three MOCFA staff, a guest curator, and the consultant.

The morning following the first advisory committee meeting, one of the SFSU faculty members who had attended the meeting called the consultant and shared many insights and thoughts. She said, "You have brought in good advisors – it looks like you have done your homework." She provided honest and insightful ideas and feedback, and the consultant realized how fortunate they were to connect with this advisor. Throughout the project, the advisor provided insights into effective ways of being with, listening to, and learning from Bay Area Native community members. She shared stories about her own experiences, providing guidance, through example, of the value of listening and respect. She participated as a teaching artist, leading a family workshop in beading and in suggesting people to connect with for the opening-day program. After the exhibition closed at MOCFA, the advisor continued to provide the consultant with guidance in connecting with advisors and the importance of valuing what an advisor brings.

In the example above, the MOCFA leadership and staff recognized the importance of learning from, and being guided by, community members whose expertise and perspectives are valued. The staff and consultant thoughtfully learned about potential advisory committee members, and they were persistent in reaching out and connecting with community members. Did they do *everything* right at the first advisory committee meeting? No, but the advisors were gracious and listened to the museum representatives. The advisors paid attention; they understood that the museum was trying to learn from and honor their perspectives and expertise. Relationships that were nurtured during the development of the exhibition and programs continued to develop in subsequent years, resulting in deeper relationships, more opportunities for advising, and additional programming.

Advisory Groups

The museum leadership and staff may be considering creating an advisory group as one of their strategies for learning about communities. Advisory groups are a very effective way to build relationships with community leaders, representatives of community organizations, and others whose perspectives will enhance the organization's activities. Advisory groups are created to serve various functions, from short-term groups that focus on specific projects to longer-term or more permanent groups. Advisory group members often assist by recommending, planning and implementing programs, recommending marketing strategies, providing the perspective of their constituencies in group discussions, and suggesting community resources for specific activities.

For any advisory group, it is critical to understand the importance of *valuing the diverse perspectives* that advisory committee members bring and for one's organization to *demonstrate a commitment to follow through*. This does not mean that the organization will have to implement every recommendation offered by advisory groups. It does mean that the staff will need to be honest about what the organization can and cannot do. It means respecting what each person brings to the group. It means creating a place for community dialogue, building relationships, nurturing collaborations, and working together to benefit the organization and the community organizations that are represented on the advisory committee.

The following strategies will assist in planning for advisory groups:

- Identify the types of advisory groups that are desirable. The groups may be focused on a variety of areas and audiences: education, specific geographic areas or communities, etc. For each advisory group, identify the types of people the staff hopes will serve on the committee. For example, if an advisory group for education is to be formed, identify the specific perspectives that the staff will want (administrators; teachers, including specific grade levels; curriculum specialists; parents). Also, identify the geographic range that the advisory group members will represent. For advisory groups centered on specific programs, identify the people who may have a specific interest in the subject of the program.
- Create a list of potential advisory group members. As in the processes outlined for identifying community stakeholders, start by looking internally at who museum leadership and staff already know. Consider whose perspectives will be most helpful and who might be most interested in serving.
- Clearly define and articulate the purpose of each advisory group. This is a crucial early step so that the museum leadership, staff, and potential advisory committee members understand their individual role and the role of the committee overall.
- Clearly identify what staff members would like advisory group members to do and what they hope the results will be. Be clear about expectations and talk about these throughout the time the advisory committee is active.
- Clearly define who will be the group's chair/facilitator, who will staff the group, how decisions will be made, who will do follow-up, etc. Clearly defining how much authority advisory committee members have, individually and collectively, is crucial, as is defining how decisions will be made and how the committee will hold its members accountable.
- Determine how often the advisory group will meet in person or by phone.
- Create a budget for each advisory group. Include honoraria for the advisors. Honoring advisors' perspectives, expertise, and experience through financial means demonstrates that they are valued.

- Finalize the list of potential advisory group members.
- Call and/or email each potential member and invite them to participate. Mention who recommended them. Describe the project, the time commitment, and that their perspective is important.
- Send a packet of information about the organization and the specific project to each person who has agreed to serve on the advisory committee.
- Schedule the first meeting.
- Remember that the community leaders who agree to serve are giving their time, expertise, and perspective. It is very important to honor and value their expertise. People want to know that they are being listened to and that their opinions are respected.

The suggested processes described in this chapter will guide the leadership and staff as they learn about their community. This is an iterative process; learning about one's community is ongoing, and everything that staff and leadership learn can help them refine the process for future learning and understanding.

Bibliography

Acevedo, S. (2013, September 18). Interculturalism: A new way of understanding audience engagement. Retrieved from http://www.contemporanea.us/2013/09/interculturalism-a-new-way-of-understanding-audience-engagement/

Bloch, M., Carter, S., & McLean, A. (n.d.). Mapping America: Every city, every block. Retrieved from http://projects.nytimes.com/census/2010/explorer

Burd-Sharps, S., & Lewis, K. (2014). *A portrait of California 2014-2015.* United States: American Human Development Project. Foreword, p. 4, Key Findings, p. 7. Retrieved from http://ssrc-static.s3.amazonaws.com/wp-content/uploads/2014/12/A-Portrait-of-California_vF.pdf

Community Facts. (n.d.). American FactFinder. Retrieved from http://factfinder2.census.gov/faces/nav/jsf/pages/index.xhtml

Introduction to Community Organizing. (n.d.). Campus Compact. Retrieved from http://compact.org/resource-posts/introduction-to-community-organizing/

Kidsdata.org. (n.d.). A program of the Lucile Packard Foundation for Children's Health. Retrieved from http://www.kidsdata.org/

Kretzmann, J. P., & McKnight, J. L. (1993). *Building communities from the inside out: A path toward finding and mobilizing a community's assets.* Chicago: ACTA Publications.

Mattessich, P., & Monsey, B. (1997). *Community building: What makes it work.* Saint Paul, MN: Amherst H. Wilder Foundation.

MediaPost News. (n.d.). Brand and product marketing: Engage target market newsletters (affluent, boomers, millennials, Hispanics, men, moms, teens). Retrieved from http://www.mediapost.com/

Nextdoor. (n.d.). Retrieved from https://nextdoor.com/

Quan, R. (2016, May 14). *Jeff Mori 2016 Kimochi Spirit Awards* [Video file]. Retrieved from https://www.youtube.com/watch?v=7dN7Ybk6GPA

State of California Department of Education. (n.d.). California school directory. Retrieved from http://www.cde.ca.gov/re/sd/

State of California Department of Finance. (n.d.). Demographic reports. Retrieved from http://www.dof.ca.gov/Reports/Demographic_Reports/

United States Census Bureau. (n.d.). Retrieved from http://www.census.gov/

Using FactFinder - Getting started with American FactFinder. (n.d.). American FactFinder. Retrieved from http://factfinder2.census.gov/faces/nav/jsf/pages/using_factfinder.xhtml

Whiteford, L., and Vindrola-Padros, C. (2015). *Community participatory involvement: A sustainable model for global health.* Walnut Creek, CA: Left Coast Press.

8

CREATING A COMMUNITY INVOLVEMENT ACTION PLAN

Learning about oneself, learning about one's museum, and learning about one's community are continual processes. The Community Involvement Action Plan brings that information together. Museum leadership and staff have collected information and reviewed how their museum accomplishes its mission, especially as it relates to priority audiences and community. Planners have done internal research with internal stakeholders, such as staff, board members, and volunteers, and external research with community members. For the internal research, the planners have identified and defined current and potential audiences, defined the museum's unique niche, and looked at what programs the museum offers and what audiences say about those programs. Using what planners learn from an institutional assessment can provide the information needed to build a Community Involvement Action Plan.

With the information and insights gained, it is time to create the strategic action plan to involve the community and the museum. The plan is intended to be relevant to the communities the museum leadership and staff have learned about and address the interests and concerns of that community and the museum. It is an action plan, to cover a three- to five-year time period, with detailed action steps for the first year and more general action steps for subsequent years.

When the leadership and staff start creating the action plan, the questions to think about are:

- What are our goals and specific strategies, including the *internal* work for the museum to do?
- Who will do it?
- What is the timeframe?
- What are the resources needed?
- How will we measure results?

A sample form to assist in this process (called Community Involvement Action Plan) is included in Appendix A.

The leadership and staff who are building this plan will start with setting goals for involving the community, articulating what they hope to achieve and aligning those goals with the museum's strategic plan. In addition, if the museum is using a theory of change model, the articulated goals from that model can be added to the CI Action Plan form. Leadership and staff need to consider the possible challenges in addressing those goals and to keep them in mind as they begin to develop the plan.

Guidelines

As leadership and staff create the plan, the following guidelines will be useful. The plan needs to:

- Include a compelling and articulate rationale for the overall plan, identifying how it serves the goals of the community and the museum. This is where the planners can include the preliminary work they have done, articulating their intentions and responses to the key questions posed at the beginning of Chapter 6. It is also where they can articulate what they learned about the community's overall interests and concerns.
- Be explicit about how the plan develops and nurtures an ongoing relationship between the museum and the community, embedding the relationship in daily practice.
- Be explicit about how it addresses specific community interests and concerns.
- Address the following:

  o What are the strategies to ensure that the museum is an integral part of the community? As part of the initial planning work, museum leadership and staff engaged in internal discussions about what it means to be an integral part of the community and the internal processes they need to put into place to make this happen. This part of the plan is where those strategies can come into play.

  o How will the museum become known in the community as a community resource that is readily used and considered? Keeping this question in mind when the leadership and staff develop the plan will help to identify specific strategies to engage in projects that are visible and are organized by well-respected community stakeholders. When the museum shows that it is a good partner in community projects, community members will come to know and trust the museum as a community resource.

  o What strategies will leadership and staff employ to ensure that the museum is "at the table" when decisions that affect the community are being discussed and made?

  o What specific community organizations will staff work with? Identifying the specific community organizations and the reasons they would be appropriate community partners is a key component of the community involvement action plan. The more specific the museum leadership and staff can be, the better.

- Include a well-conceived rationale for each of the action steps proposed (i.e., *why* is that action being proposed?).
- Include a timeline for the action steps and an indication of who will be involved in each step. (A sample form, called Community Involvement Action Timeline, is included in Appendix A.)
- Include a detailed chart of goals, strategies, resources needed, and timeframe. (A sample form, called Community Involvement Action Plan, is included in Appendix A.) For each primary action, include evaluation strategies to measure progress as the plan proceeds. For example, will staff members develop surveys for program participants? Will they conduct interviews with key community stakeholders to identify possible follow-up actions? Consider what evaluation strategies will provide information that can be used to refine the programs that are recommended. These evaluation strategies will inform staff members' practice so they can adjust programs and actions as needed.
- Include a list of community resources, organizations, and leaders, with their contact information, so other museum staff members can follow up with the contacts that were initiated. (A sample form, called Community Involvement Master Contact List, is included in Appendix A.)

Areas to Be Addressed in the Community Involvement Action Plan

Using the guidelines noted above, the leadership and staff will address the following organizational components, ensuring that the plan aligns with the organization's strategic plan. The team that is developing the community involvement action plan will consult with museum leadership and staff to determine which areas are of highest priority. The following questions can help guide the planning process for each area.

- *Administration*: Include specifics on how the museum's administration will support community involvement. What strategies will the museum's leadership develop to become more community responsive? Will new positions be created? Will current position descriptions be rewritten to reflect a stronger emphasis on community work? Will staff training and professional development strategies be included, and will funds be allocated for this? Will there be new board responsibilities, new or revamped advisory committees? How will the museum's leadership and staff interact with the leadership in the community? The examples included in the Stories from the Field sections throughout this book describe many ways that other organizations have addressed these questions.
- *Development/funding strategies*: Include specifics on how the museum's development staff will support community involvement. How will the plan be

funded? What will be the responsibility of the community, and what will be the responsibility of the museum? How will the costs of long-term community involvement be incorporated into the museum's and partnering organizations' regular operating budgets? These are critical questions to address, particularly the question about planning for long-term community involvement. How will the museum build in sustainability so it is part of regular operating costs, not a separate grant-funded initiative?

- *Curatorial and collections management*: Include specifics on how the museum's curatorial and collections management staff will support community involvement. How will the staff begin working with community leaders to identify potential additions to the collection? How will staff help members of the community see that their artifacts and records are important and that the museum is truly interested in collecting them? Will the museum collect oral histories, and, if so, how will staff and community members be trained to do so? What access will the museum provide to community members so they can see/ visit/use their items after they become part of the museum? How will the museum determine which items to add to the collection? Will staff incorporate some items as part of a teaching collection? What policies will museum leadership and staff adopt to encourage collecting in the community? There are many complex questions to address with a collections focus, and those noted above are a good place to start the conversation and planning.

- *Exhibitions*: Include specifics on how the museum's exhibitions staff will support community involvement. Will the museum develop one or more exhibitions? If so, what are the core messages of these exhibition(s)? Will community partners be part of the exhibition development process? Describe the ways that staff will work with community partners. Will the exhibition(s) be developed by the staff or developed jointly with community participation? What are the strategies to ensure full community ownership of the exhibition(s)? Will diverse community perspectives be incorporated in the exhibition's text and interpretive material? What processes will staff use to build and nurture relationships with community stakeholders? Will staff conduct community workshops with community groups? Will leadership and staff create a community advisory committee? How will the exhibition content and specific messages address the interests and concerns of the community?

- *Programming*: Include specifics on how the museum's programming staff will support community involvement. Describe the programs in the plan, and clearly articulate the ways that staff members will work with their community partners. Will the programs be developed jointly with community participation? What are the strategies to ensure full community ownership of the programs? Will diverse community perspectives be incorporated into the programs? What are the core messages of the programs? How do the programs address the interests and concerns of the community? What processes will staff use to build and nurture relationships with stakeholders? Will staff conduct community workshops with community groups? Will leadership and staff create a community advisory committee?

- *Marketing and publicity*: Include specifics on how the museum's marketing staff will support community involvement. How will staff work with community members to identify appropriate marketing strategies? How will leadership and staff determine who takes care of which responsibilities? Who is the priority audience, and how did the museum's leadership and staff determine that? What will be the short- and long-term publicity strategies? Which publications will be the primary focus? What are the goals of the publicity and marketing efforts? How will staff measure whether the museum attains those goals?

As the museum leadership and staff develop the plan, it is important to include how they plan to sustain projects so they are not one-time-only events but rather build on one another. *Build sustainability into the plan.* This starts with an action plan, but it will build over the years. Realize, too, that the future is unpredictable. Even when leadership and staff have done their due diligence and have a theory of change, they can't always predict what will happen. They are developing connections and relationships with people for the long term, so they may not be able to plan on specific outcomes. When the leadership and staff are committed and the relationships they are developing are based on respect and mutual trust, they will be more resilient and able to learn from each experience.

Strategies to Incorporate into the Plan

Community involvement is labor intensive and works best if everyone in the museum is actively involved. The team that creates the community involvement action plan will incorporate specific action steps. As the team members consider what those will be, there are suggested strategies for involving everyone and leveraging community connections. They include the following:

Museum–Community Liaisons and Advocates

Museum leaders and staff may want to be more community involved but might not have sufficient time to do all they'd like. The museum's volunteers could be well suited for carrying on some of the community involvement work. Leadership and staff may want to work with the volunteers to empower them to be advocates for the museum in the community and advocates for the community in the museum. If they do create a way for volunteers to serve as museum–community liaisons and advocates, they will want to consider the following as they plan:

- *Training*: The museum–community liaisons and advocates will need to be fully informed about the museum and its programs and be able to articulate why the museum is interested in connecting with the specific community and serving community members more fully. This will likely mean that the liaisons and advocates will go through training. Effective training will include information about the museum, its goals and plans, and *why* they are interested in community work. It will also include training and support about working with community members and community groups. Working with trainers who specialize in community organizing will be useful for the museum–community liaisons and advocates and for the museum staff.

- *Influence and power*: As this program is being developed, the museum leadership will need to determine the level of influence the museum–community liaisons and advocates will have. Empowering the volunteers to act on behalf of the museum in specific ways will be beneficial. This can range from being able to offer free meeting space for community groups, to giving discounted/free admission to specific groups, offering behind-the-scenes tours, and providing publicity for community events that the museum is co-sponsoring. The leadership will want to determine what types of services the museum–community liaisons and advocates can offer to community groups and how much authority they feel comfortable delegating to volunteers. The intent is to open up the museum so that all the community groups feel connected with it and know someone associated with it.

- *Advocacy and connection*: The volunteer museum–community liaisons and advocates can serve as conduits between the museum and community. When a request is made that is beyond their authority, they know whom to go to and how to facilitate the connection between the museum staff and the community. A pilot program might start with the museum's current volunteers who are already very familiar with the institution, such as docents, information desk volunteers, and welcomers/hosts. They are people who are experienced in interacting with the public and know how to engage people in conversation. The pilot program would identify a few key community organizations to begin with and later expand as more connections and networking naturally occur.

- The museum–community liaisons and advocates could also participate in community meetings, learning about current interests and concerns within communities, finding community voices, and bringing those voices to the attention of museum leadership and staff. In this way, there are more person-to-person connections, leading to strengthened relationships.

Community Partnerships

Creating partnerships with community organizations is an effective way to establish and nurture the relationships with community members. Much has been written about the process of creating and implementing partnerships, including *Culture Builds Communities: A Guide to Partnership Building and Putting Culture to Work on Social Issues* from Partners for Livable Communities, *Urban Network: Museums Embracing Communities, Collaboration: Critical Criteria for Success* from the Pacific Science Center, and *Museums in the Life of a City: Strategies for Community Partnerships*. A Blade of Grass (ABOG) is an organization that nurtures and supports socially engaged art, often in partnership with museums and cultural organizations, and ABOG has created a set of guidelines for artists and cultural organizations seeking their support. ABOG's Reports from the Field is a series of forums with perspectives from the artists and their experiences with the program. These perspectives help to inform program planners as they plan partnerships.

A summary of the attributes and actions that characterize effective partnerships will serve as a guideline and reminder for organizations as they establish partnerships. Successful partnerships are often characterized by the following:

- They are built on already established relationships. The people and organizations establish relationships with one another first, well before the idea of a partnership arises. Collaborations are more likely to succeed if there is a trusting relationship already established.
- In effective partnerships, each partnering organization has clarified its *goals and expectations* and the goals and expectations of the primary people who will be involved. What does each potential partner hope will happen as a result of the partnership? What are the expectations of each partnering organization? The leadership and staff of each partnering organization will clearly describe these. A number of conversations may take place while the expectations and goals are being clarified. These conversations will also focus on clearly identifying roles and responsibilities of the partnership organizations and key individuals.
- In effective partnerships, key individuals become familiar with the work style and culture of potential partners. They respect the philosophy, pace, and resources of the partnering organizations.
- Partnering organizations have related missions. When a cultural organization is considering potential partners, it focuses on organizations whose mission is related to its own organizational mission.
- In effective partnerships, partners develop the *overall goals and purpose* for the project together. Each organization may have a different reason for entering into a partnership, but it is important that all partners work toward a common purpose. Partners also develop goals that are flexible and appropriate to the partners' missions and resources.
- Successful partnerships often begin with smaller projects, building in a high chance for success. This also serves to plant the seed for future collaborations.
- In effective partnerships, the partners understand that collaborations often proceed slowly, and they know that these projects take time. They understand the time commitment and see the long-term benefits.
- Successful partnerships include developing a plan for ongoing evaluation of the project as well as evaluation of the collaboration process itself. The evaluation plan includes opportunities to reflect on the collaboration process and adjust accordingly.
- Effective partnerships are *balanced* in actions and strategies. As an example, partners might alternate meeting sites so that each partner can host and involve more of its staff when the meeting is at its site.

- Effective partnerships are built on developing trusting relationships with individuals and organizations. Many of the attributes and characteristics discussed in Chapter 6, such as paying attention to one's assumptions, humility, patience and tenacity, empathy, and the ability to truly listen, are relevant and integral to developing these trusting relationships.
- In successful partnerships, decision making is shared. In the early stages of the partnership, partners discuss how decisions will be made. Throughout the partnership, partners will reflect on the decision-making and collaboration process and adjust accordingly so that the process they have developed continues to work for each partner.
- Because successful partnerships are based on trusting relationships, the partners focus on the *process* of the partnership. This does not mean that the products, such as programs and exhibitions, are not important. It does mean that the process of working together is crucial.
- In effective partnerships, especially those involving organizations of different sizes, acknowledging the different levels of resources available from each organization is important. Effective partnership projects are conducted in an equitable and balanced manner. If larger organizations have more resources to contribute to a project, that does not change the balance. Every partner contributes according to its ability, and they all receive equal credit and recognition.
- In many instances, it is a good idea to formalize the partnership through a memo of understanding. This is another way to clarify expectations, roles, and responsibilities.
- In effective partnerships, the key individuals who are working together realize that there may be rough spots along the way, just as there are in any relationship. These individuals, and their partnership organizations, commit to working through these rough spots with one another so that the partnership continues to thrive.

This summary of the attributes and actions that characterize effective partnerships is a reminder for organizations as they establish partnerships. The resources noted at the beginning of this section provide more specific guidance and lessons about partnerships and collaborations.

The Importance of Face-to-Face Interaction

One of the most important outcomes of creating and implementing a Community Involvement Action Plan is for people in the museum to form and nurture long-lasting, trusting relationships with people in the community. This is best done face to face. Emails and phone calls are convenient and important communication tools, but it is not effective to rely on them to the exclusion of meeting with people in person. Trust is developed when someone spends time with others, so go out and meet with people. Spend time with them, share a meal together, and get to know them.

Recognize that creating and maintaining personal relationships with community members is the most effective way to build support. The National Awareness, Attitudes and Usage Study conducted by IMPACTS Research and the Monterey Bay Aquarium found that for donors (supporters), personal communication is key to continuing support. The simple act of thanking a supporter goes a long way toward letting someone know that they matter and are appreciated.

Creating a welcoming space, not just at the entrance but throughout the institution, sets the plan in motion. Chapter 3 included a discussion on invitation – that invitation is the means through which hospitality is created. Creating a welcoming space is integral to this.

Stories from the Field: Brooklyn Historical Society

The Brooklyn Historical Society (BHS) is an urban history center in a landmark building completed in 1881. It is a cultural hub and a place for civic dialogue. Deborah Schwartz, president of the society, has described BHS as a "go-to" place for public discussion. How has this come about? There were a number of changes that Schwartz instigated at BHS, including taking out the big permanent exhibit, which freed up critical space and enabled BHS to create a flexible, comfortable place for people to gather and have a conversation. In 2010, the BHS engaged in a strategic planning process that resulted in an aspirational new vision – to tie history to the present and future and to create a program that was inclusive and expansive in its breadth, covering a range of ideas, historical and contemporary. As Schwartz notes, "We hoped people would think of us as the 92nd Street Y, Brooklyn style. We wanted to be a place that showcases intellectuals and scholars and at the same time we wanted our audiences to feel that they were central to the experience of attending our programs." This has resulted in steadily increasing attendance. People come to BHS because they know they will find dialogue and conversation.

The changes in the physical space overlapped with changes in staffing that included hiring a full-time oral historian and eventually resulted in the hiring of a team of public programmers. Collecting oral history interviews creates opportunities to connect to people throughout the incredibly diverse neighborhoods of Brooklyn. In 2011 BHS undertook an ambitious project called *Crossing Borders, Bridging Generations*, organized by oral historian Sady Sullivan. Focused on people who self-identify as being of mixed heritage, the project required BHS staff to connect more deeply with people and communities who may not have known about them before.

BHS staff created programming in community spaces, working with community members to train them in interviewing, fanning out to neighborhoods throughout the borough. A diverse team conducted over one hundred interviews, and the project has resulted in oral histories posted on the *Crossing Borders, Bridging Generations* website, an array of public programs, an educational curriculum, and published scholarly essays. The project is complete, but it has provided numerous opportunities to connect with a wide-ranging audience and to forge partnerships with other organizations. The oral histories are catalogued and available online and have become an important collection available for use by scholars in the years to come.

Crossing Borders, Bridging Generations also spurred new program formats, including the "What Are You?" program, a conversation with a facilitator about difficult issues commonly faced by people of mixed heritage. *Crossing Borders* also resulted in numerous partnerships with other organizations, including the Loving Day Project, the Arab American Association of New York, Race Forward, and Swirl. BHS has seen the power of program that is shaped around the pressing needs and interests of its diverse audience. Over time, BHS has become a place not only to learn but to listen and be heard. People are encouraged to speak up, to engage, and to listen respectfully to others. This participatory approach to program has become an expectation of the audience – "I can be part of this conversation," remarked one regular participant at a *Crossing Borders* event. Schwartz notes, "Our staff keeps their eye on currents in the news and in the Borough of Brooklyn, and takes the pulse of visitors who attend programs. We try to stay nimble and responsive to the issues facing our communities" (D. Schwartz, personal communication, September 25, 2015).

The Brooklyn Historical Society is creating a welcoming space. The physical surroundings, the staffing, and the programming are impacting public expectations and the public experience. The *Crossing Borders, Bridging Generations* project is a clear example of welcoming people who may not feel welcome in other settings. The change that Schwartz noted – the idea that "I can be part of this conversation" – indicates that the sense of welcoming is pervading BHS and positively impacting its community.

The power of welcoming is one of the most potent attributes that museums can embrace. A sense of welcoming underpins many overt and covert aspects of inclusive museum operations and culture. It is evident in the inclusive museum's publicity, social media, and marking materials. It is evident in the physical approach to the museum, and it is evident upon entering the museum. Museum staff and leadership can ask themselves, "What does it feel like when people enter our museum? Are they greeted by someone near the entrance with a warm smile and a hello? Do the people at the front desk greet each person and sincerely communicate that they are glad the person is there? Do our staff members seem to genuinely enjoy being here and connecting with our visitors?" If the answers are yes, the museum is already demonstrating a sense of welcome.

The next example, Thanksgiving Point Institute, highlights an organization that considers, learns about, and involves its communities as it focuses on being a good neighbor.

Stories from the Field: Thanksgiving Point Institute

Thanksgiving Point Institute in Lehi, Utah, is a farm, garden, and museum complex that draws upon the natural world to cultivate transformative family learning. Lorie Millward, Vice President of Design and Programming, shares how Thanksgiving Point is actively learning about and involving its communities:

Our challenge was that our programs were not adequately serving some of our communities. To address this, we had to figure out what they needed from us. So we did a lot of listening, and a lot of relationship-building, understanding that if we wanted people to show up for us, we needed to show up for them. We recognized that we needed to develop mutually beneficial relationships, not just so we could say that we reached a particular segment of our community, or that we offer programs to X, Y, and Z populations. It's not about seeing ourselves as the center of the community; it's about being *part* of the neighborhood, being a good neighbor and building relationships that are trusting, that are foundational and deep – so that they don't die when people leave jobs. It's a lot of work that takes time and commitment. It takes reflection and introspection. It takes realignment of some of the business goals, too, recognizing that there's a value to the social bottom line, as well as the financial bottom line, and working to ensure that those are not in conflict with one another. A perpetual issue is knowing *why* it's important to the institution to be an inclusive neighbor. Is it important in order to access more funding? Is it important in order to feel good about what the organization is giving to the community? Or is it important because as a part of the community we understand the needs of our neighbors? We sincerely want to be a good neighbor and contribute in authentic ways.

We develop programs in tandem with community members. Not simply providing them with our ideas and saying, "We'll develop this program for you, and that should fill your needs," but, "Come sit around the table with us, help us figure this out, what do you want to see, how can we make that happen, who in your community would like to be involved? What programs or initiatives do you have that we can help with?" so that programs are based on relationships, and reflective of our shared goals and aspirations.

An example of one such program is Operation Inquiry. It was developed with parents, teachers, and counselors from our local junior and high schools. We are in an area of the state where residents enjoy a nice standard of living, but that doesn't mean that everybody in the community has what they need to get by. We also have some marginalized groups, folks from diverse cultural backgrounds, and we hear from parents and teachers that a lot of kids are academically at risk because of social issues, or challenging situations in their lives. So the schools and the parents really helped us to understand who *they* wanted to serve, and then we worked together to develop Operation Inquiry, an out-of-school-time "maker" program that involves students identified by parents, counselors, and teachers to be at risk in some way. The goal of the program is to help these kids build their technical skillsets to prepare them for jobs, higher education, and careers in the STEM industries that surround the Thanksgiving Point area.

Kids come every day after school and throughout the summer to work on "maker" kinds of things. Some work on electronics, some work on micro-technology and biotech, others work on video and film production or cosplay costumes – whatever their interest is. They learn, not just how to use cool tech and tools, but also about design thinking and innovative problem solving. They learn how to use empathy to understand what others need or how a solution or product might impact the final user. They learn how to work with others and how developing relationships allows them to communicate more effectively and work through opposing opinions and problems.

The impactful thing about this program is that it brought kids who were struggling in some way together, and they formed their own community. Kids that were feeling marginalized at school, that didn't have many trusted friends, are now in a program with others who may have felt the same way, and it's a safe environment for them to share their struggles, to support and help one another. We've seen some incredible changes in many of the kids in this very way – teens with learning differences who felt ashamed at school, and have retreated inward because of that, starting to come out of their shells. We keep in touch with and involve the parents in the program, so that we can gauge whether and how their teens are benefitting. In some cases, the parents of these kids are working multiple jobs, or may not know how to help their children with some of their issues, so involving them in the program is essential to support those kids and their families. We've seen a great little community develop around this. Student grades shot up almost instantly, and their social skills (for those who are struggling with that) improved. It's wonderful to hear somebody like our sweet Gabe say, "I don't feel safe asking my questions at school, but you guys are my friends, so I'm going to ask you."

Our goal was to help at-risk kids develop marketable skills so that they could be prepared to enter the STEM education pipeline and workforce. That was the goal *we* had, the goal of parents, teachers, and counselors too. But, of course, the kids brought their own agendas, and got out of the program what they needed,

That was an important take-away and encouraged us to collaborate with more neighbors. We continually refine our processes and work to ensure that we are establishing safe environments that promote connection, stimulate discussion, and allow for failure to happen. More importantly, we are able to deepen our relationship as neighbors as we work alongside them and facilitate meaningful interactions with their families.

L. Millward, personal communication, April 15, 2016

It is clear that many of the attributes discussed in Chapter 6 (wholeheartedness, empathy, the ability to truly listen, and humility) are at play at Thanksgiving Point. It is also clear that the leadership and staff are focusing on intention – about why it is important for the institution to be an inclusive neighbor. The key questions raised at the beginning of Chapter 6 are being asked in concrete ways at Thanksgiving Point, and the ongoing discussions to try to answer these questions are guiding the museum in its community involvement practices. The description of the museum's practice – "Come sit around the table with us and help us figure this out" – is an example of a wholehearted approach that is focused on listening, learning, and connecting. Museum staff *listen* to community members, and *together* they develop programs that address community concerns. The Operation Inquiry program is one example of how this plays out, and there are numerous other examples, at Thanksgiving Point and elsewhere, that demonstrate the effectiveness of this approach.

Continuing the Connection Through Thick and Thin

Continuing a relationship or collaboration can be a challenge, especially when there are staff changes at the museum or partnering organization. When that happens, how do leadership and staff continue to nurture the relationship? If the person who is leaving has strong relationships with individuals in the community, they can share information with the museum's leadership about the community people and projects with whom they are involved. The leadership team can identify who will have the responsibility of continuing the relationships and partnerships, and the staff person who is leaving will introduce the new person to people in the community. Relationships are based on person-to-person contact, so it's important to get the relationship with the new person off to the right start. The new staff members will focus on developing their own relationships with community members. This lets community members know that the museum is still interested in working with them and is committed to developing a relationship. It lets community people know that they are still welcome.

Bibliography

A Blade of Grass. (n.d.) About the fellowship. Retrieved from http://www.abladeofgrass.org/fellowship-program/

A Blade of Grass. (n.d.) Reports from the field. Retrieved from http://www.abladeofgrass.org/reports-from-the-field/

Hirzy, E. (ed.). (1995). *Museums in the life of a city: Strategies for community partnerships.* Washington, DC: American Association of Museums.

IMPACTS Research and Monterey Bay Aquarium. (n.d.). National Awareness, Attitudes and Usage Study. Retrieved from https://impactsnaau.wordpress.com/

Kadoyama, M. (2010, May). *Sing me your story community connections project: Monthly lessons from the field May 2007–April/May 2010.* California Exhibition Resources Alliance. Available upon request from the author.

Pacific Science Center and SLi. (1997). *Collaboration: Critical criteria for success.* Washington, DC: Association of Science-Technology Centers.

Partners for Livable Communities. (1995). *Culture builds communities: A guide to partnership building and putting culture to work on social issues.* Washington, DC: Partners for Livable Communities.

Schwartz, D. (2015, January 6). *A museum director reflects on #MuseumsrespondtoFerguson* [Blog post]. Retrieved from http://www.museumcommons.com/2015/01/museum-director-reflects-museumsrespondtoferguson.html

Spitz, J. A., & Thom, M. (Ed.). (2003). *Urban network: Museums embracing communities.* Chicago: Field Museum. Distributed by The University of Chicago Press. Retrieved from http://amdurspitz.com/about-us/resources/

PART III

Challenges, Outcomes, Impacts, and Accountability

What challenges and potential outcomes and impacts might museums face when connecting deeply with their communities? Desirable outcomes and impacts are much more likely when there is accountability. What forms should this take? As museum–community involvement potentially changes organizations and communities in significant ways, this is not really the end but rather part of a circular and growing process. Museum–community involvement is not a linear process. It is not "Do step 1 and this will happen. Do step 2 and this will happen." Relationships among people, even relationships that seem simple, are complex, and leadership and staff are encouraged to embrace ambiguity and complexity.

How can museums approach change so it is long lasting, not occasional or temporary? As organizations start and continue to embrace community, how will they sustain this? Staff and board members come and go, and what is important to one executive director, CEO, or board chair may not be as important to the next. So a community involvement initiative may languish. Perhaps when an organization receives a lot of attention, publicity, and press for its community engagement, it becomes more sustainable, as there is pressure to maintain the reason for the attention. The first chapter in Part 3 addresses challenges – and there will be challenges.

PART III

Challenges, Outcomes, Impacts, and Accountability

9
CHALLENGES

Museum–community involvement work encompasses people and the complexity of relationships so that, even when people are wholehearted, have listened and planned thoroughly, and are developing and nurturing relationships with community stakeholders, there are challenges. Perhaps, as staff members connect with people and develop relationships, they learn that there are sharp divisions within the community. They may have had a heads-up about this as they began learning about the community but thought that they wouldn't need to address the internal divisions and groups. Sometimes, even with the best intentions, while staff members are building trusting relationships with various stakeholders and community members they find themselves and their museum in a challenging situation. Chapter 6 discussed the importance of bravery and courage in getting started. This chapter addresses courage and what to do when things go awry. This is where museum leadership and staff have to step up and where they can look for and find the support they need to learn and move forward.

Stories from the Field: Science Museum of Minnesota

An example of some very real challenges in community work is the story of the Science Museum of Minnesota (SMM) and its experience with *RACE: Are We So Different?*, a project of the American Anthropological Association and developed by the Science Museum of Minnesota. The Science Museum of Minnesota is a large science museum in St. Paul, and its exhibitions and programs reflect its values, which include serving a vital role in its community. The *RACE: Are We So Different?* exhibition opened at SMM in January 2007 and since then has traveled to more than fifty institutions.

On July 6, 2016, Philando Castile was fatally shot by a police officer in a suburb of St. Paul, near where the SMM is located. Joanne Jones-Rizzi, director of

Community Engagement at the time (and currently vice president of STEM Equity & Education) at the Science Museum of Minnesota, shares the story:

> I went in to work, and everybody was stunned. The event happened several miles from the museum – not very far – and it really felt like this was very close to home. The President of the museum [Alison Brown, SMM President and CEO] was present and very visible, talking with staff. We have the RACE exhibition in residence now, and there was this sense that we wanted to do something, but we weren't clear on what. People felt very vulnerable, and it felt very raw. And upsetting. There was this sense of "What can we do?"
>
> I communicated with some community groups and said that if they wanted a space to process what had happened, that we would make the space available for them in the museum.
>
> This was all done informally. We were trying to figure out what we could do. Alison wanted me to write a statement to put in the exhibition. She was communicating with the staff, with thoughtful messages, acknowledging our individual and collective pain.
>
> I wrote a statement, from the perspective of the staff and Board, and I sent it to Alison. Alison sent it to the board and they approved it. We installed it in the entrance to the *RACE* exhibition so that visitors could see it when they entered.
>
> The statement read:
>
> "Thank you for visiting *RACE: Are We So Different?* The staff and Board of the Science Museum of Minnesota join the community in mourning the tragic killing of Philando Castile. While we don't have answers on how to heal, we hope that taking time to learn and talk with others about the history of race in our country and the systemic issues of racism as presented within our exhibition provides a deeper context for understanding the impact of race and racism on each of us individually and as a society.
>
> "For further resources visit understandingrace.org."
>
> I felt it was a compassionate statement. It was serious, because it acknowledged the death of a human being. The staff who work in the exhibit are all trained, and receive ongoing training to talk with people about these kinds of issues. I also sent the statement to the head of the Saint Paul police department, as I wanted him to know that this statement was going up. He responded, "I don't have a problem with this. Thank you for sending it to me."
>
> We put the statement in the exhibition on Friday, July 15, 2016. The following Wednesday, the wife of a police officer, from a neighboring community, came into the exhibition and saw that statement. She felt very strongly that the statement was anti-law enforcement and she wanted to talk with somebody. I was out of town, so she met with Alison. She also took a photograph of the statement and sent it via social media to law enforcement family pages, like Facebook pages, saying that the Science Museum was anti-law enforcement.

> # Thank you for visiting
> ## *RACE: Are We So Different?*
>
> ## The staff and Board of the Science Museum of Minnesota join the community in mourning the tragic killing of Philando Castile.
>
> While we don't have answers on how to heal, we hope that taking time to learn and talk with others about the history of race in our country and the systemic issues of racism as presented within our exhibition provides a deeper context for understanding the impact of race and racism on each of us individually and as a society.
>
> For further resources visit
> understandingrace.org

FIGURE 9.1 Science Museum of Minnesota statement on shooting of Philando Castile. Photo: Bryan Kennedy.

The impact was immediate. Within minutes, the membership office and the Museum's call center started receiving phone calls complaining about the sign.

Alison, the Director of PR, and I talked about how to best respond. I wasn't there to fully understand how upset people were. Alison said that she was going to have the sign removed, because she felt the need to support the front of the house staff.

The next day an article appeared in the local Saint Paul newspaper, the Pioneer Press, with a copy of the photograph and the text of what the sign said. The museum was inundated by calls and letters from members, saying that they were proud of us for having this statement up, that this is what the museum is about, and others who said that taking down the sign was the right thing to do.

Numerous staff members were very upset when the sign came down. Alison acknowledged that and invited staff to communicate with her. Many staff members wrote eloquent letters to her, saying why they felt the statement should have remained up. They said things like, "We have people who disagree with our perspective about climate change, and people who disagree with our perspective on evolution, and we don't change exhibits based on those critiques." Alison was responsive to the staff's concerns, and we held several staff meetings where she explained the sequence of events and took full responsibility for her decision. She met with the Community Engagement group, where staff was able to share why they were upset. They felt that it was their job to create and sustain relationships with communities – all communities – and that taking the sign down jeopardized those relationships, our credibility and our reputation. They also felt that they could have helped temper some of the hostility coming from law enforcement supporters had they known. Some staff were upset that they weren't involved in the decision to take it down, or put it up. Others did not like the fact that I had written from the staff without their consent.

We created a Dialogue Station in a staff-only area, and it's still there [December 2016], where we have a chronology of the events of what happened, the statement, a copy of the newspaper article, and an editorial written by a well-known community member. We pose the question – "Why do you think the sign elicited such a strong response?" Staff have left many responses to the question.

That's where we are now [December 2016]. We are waiting to hear if the police officer will be charged. The County Attorney recently announced that the police officer will be charged for manslaughter. Alison sent an email to the staff, letting them know what had happened, and reminding them about the Dialogue Station.

It's been a very hard time for us at the Museum. The statement has been the source of numerous really good conversations – about race, about law enforcement, and about the vulnerability of people of color – particularly men of color. It has also made us aware that the *RACE* exhibition needs to be updated to reflect events taking place throughout the country between communities of color and law enforcement and about the criminal justice system.

We've learned a lot about ourselves. I was reminded that not all people share my beliefs and values. I thought we were doing something that addressed a horrible event, providing visitors and staff with a place where they could think about and process it, and put it within the context of the *RACE* exhibition. I learned that it's not that simple. And I know better! I am reminded of how complex these issues are. I don't know that we're over it yet, and taking down the dialogue station now feels like we are letting down Philando.

We are in the process now of developing a museum statement on Equity and Inclusion. This statement will be parallel to other Science Museum of Minnesota statements on Climate Change and Evolution.

J. Jones-Rizzi, personal communication, December 2, 2016

The lessons learned at the Science Museum of Minnesota echo several points made earlier: Community work and human relationships are complex, the importance of not making assumptions, the importance of person-to-person communication, and that flexibility is key. It is also important to acknowledge that challenges will happen and museum leadership and staff will need to be courageous and committed to working through them with their communities.

Stories from the Field: Arab American National Museum

The Arab American National Museum in Dearborn, Michigan, is courageously addressing its own challenges. Devon Akmon, director of the museum, describes them:

As the Arab American National Museum, we represent many people. Arabs come from 22 different countries, from waves upon waves of immigration, going back over 150 years. There's diversity in terms of religious affiliation. So it is not a singular story within the Arab American community, it's a collection of stories. We're not a monolithic group, and to try to share and reflect the diversity of that community is a challenge, especially at this time. We're dealing with war, conflict, and displacement in our homelands, so we're operating in an environment right now where there's a lot of hostility, misunderstanding, and a lot of diversity within our own community to address that story.

In addition, immigration to our nation from the Arab world has changed drastically since 2001. We're seeing more individuals coming from Arab countries in North Africa. The majority of our historical story has been largely told through the lens of the Levant – Syrian, Lebanese, Iraqi – and now we're starting to see Sudanese, Somali, Moroccan, Egyptian, and their narrative is not as well represented. We need to be responsive to these new communities.

One example of how we are addressing this is with the exhibition *Little Syria, NY: An Immigrant Community's Life & Legacy*. The first sizeable Arab American community in our nation lived in the Lower West Side of Manhattan. We are bringing the exhibition to the Ellis Island National Museum of Immigration, and it opens in October. The exhibition responds to two things: 1) portraying our community story with an accurate depiction, and 2) addressing the anti-immigrant rhetoric that is evident in public discourse. It also addresses the very complex story that's taking place in New York about the presence of Arabs in lower Manhattan. We're trying to humanize our stories, to put them in context of the greater American narrative, and to combat these larger channels of what we perceive as misinformation.

D. Akmon, personal communication, August 31, 2016

The real challenges that the Arab American National Museum is addressing, especially the rhetoric surrounding immigration and the complexities of Arab American communities, require the museum leadership and staff to step up – to actively advocate for and be responsive to their communities.

One of the most challenging aspects of involving communities that museums need to grapple with is the balance of one's own institutional voice and the voices of one's communities. When and to what degree do the museum leadership and staff impose their institutional voice, and when do they let go of that voice so that community members' voices take precedence? This is an ongoing consideration. It requires flexibility and the ability to understand the nuances of community voices and concerns as well as the nuances of institutional concerns. There are lessons to be learned from those who are actively working to make museums inclusive, including the important practice of stepping back so that community voices have the space to be in front.

What are the most effective ways to approach significant challenges? Step up, look for, and find the support one needs to learn and move forward. Use the skills and attributes discussed in Chapter 6. Be thoughtful, humble, and courageous. Consider who can help leadership and staff effectively address this challenge, bring them into the process, and ask for help. No one person can do it alone, and collectively addressing challenges will often be more effective.

Vu Le, in his November 14, 2016, blogpost "7 Agreements for Productive Conversations During Difficult Times" provides helpful guidance for addressing interpersonal challenges. These guidelines include thoughtful suggestions for considerate conduct, such as being patient with one another; providing feedback on actions and opinions, *not* on perceived motivation or character; assuming good intentions and acknowledging the impact of one's words; recognizing that someone doesn't fully understand another's reality; being gracious in accepting difficult feedback and forgiving ourselves and one another; and staying with it – not giving up when it gets difficult.

Bibliography

Le, Vu. (2016, November 14). 7 agreements for productive conversations during difficult times [Blog post]. Retrieved from http://nonprofitwithballs.com/2016/11/7-agreements-for-productive-conversations-during-difficult-times/

Science Museum of Minnesota. (n.d.). *RACE: Are we so different?* Tour schedule. Retrieved from http://www.understandinggrace.org/about/tour.html

10

OUTCOMES, IMPACTS, AND ACCOUNTABILITY

Museum–community involvement is based on relationships. Quantifying levels of trust in a relationship is not easy. How will museum leadership, staff, and community members know when a museum is truly involved with, and trusted by, its community? What might be some indicators? Consider the behaviors, actions, or events that might indicate a more extensive or deeper connection and relationship with community members. Evaluating community involvement initiatives at a museum keeps these indicators in mind.

Collective impact, as introduced in Chapter 2, focuses on cross sector collaboration to address complex social problems. In collective impact, the organizations participating in a project track progress using the same measures, collecting the same types of data, and using the same consistent methods of reporting. Collective impact is one of many approaches to evaluating outcomes and impacts of community involvement initiatives. With ongoing effective evaluation, indicators are tracked regularly and there are processes in place to make adjustments as needed. Effective community involvement happens more readily when evaluation data is used to inform program design and implementation.

Possible Outcomes and Impacts of Connecting with One's Local Community

Incorporating evaluation into the planning and implementation process positions the museum to learn about program outcomes and impacts. In planning, consider the following questions:

- What do you hope will happen as a result of having done this project? Include everything you can think of, and be specific. For example, even if you initially know very few of your local community members, consider setting a goal of having just one or two of them attend a program or reception, getting to know at least one community person better so that you can feel comfortable calling them in the future. Revisit this question throughout the process to help guide actions, so that you consistently keep the outcomes and impacts in mind. The more clearly the outcomes and impacts are articulated, the more readily the path forward will be illuminated.

- How will you know whether the outcomes and impacts you identified above have happened? Think about how you can collect information about these. For example, if you don't know community members, you might put a guest book out and introduce yourself to the people who come to your receptions and programs. Review the names and comments in the guest book. Also consider what other methods you already use to evaluate learning for your other exhibitions, and adapt those.

One of the biggest challenges for community involvement is figuring out what can be measured – what indicates whether your relationships have broadened and/or deepened? Is it the number of times you call someone to ask their advice? The number of community members you add to your email distribution list? For each outcome and impact you hope to achieve, design methods to collect the data that will serve as indicators.

Qualitative indicators might include the *number* of community members or organizations who you would feel comfortable asking for advice regarding future exhibitions, programs, or publicity; the *degree* of the relationship; *how often* you interact with community members; *how often* you are actively involved in meetings called by community organizers; *how often* you are invited to be at the table when community concerns are being discussed; and to *what degree* you are planning to engage in new collaborative projects with community members. The explicit answers to these questions might be quantitative (i.e., how many, how often, etc.), but they are indicators of deeper answers. Considering one's comfort level in calling a specific person to ask their advice or perspective is one way to look at the level of trust in the relationship.

Another way to engage in outcomes and impacts is to consider significant events that cannot be quantitatively measured, but you know that the event is pivotal and reflects a deeper relationship. Consider what these significant events mean to both the museum leadership and staff, and to the community. What makes the event significant? Does it indicate a sense of community respect and welcoming? Will staff engage community members even more deeply after this event?

These are difficult questions to ponder and answer, and it is often helpful to apply strategic methods when seeking the answers. The following examples highlight how a few organizations are considering and addressing outcomes and impacts.

Stories from the Field: Children's Museum Pittsburgh

The Children's Museum Pittsburgh (CMP), located in Pittsburgh's Northside neighborhood, is a vital community resource that provides exhibits and programs for learning and play. Among CMP's key values are a commitment to good design principles, a "play with real stuff" design philosophy, and a commitment to diversity.

Chris Siefert, formerly deputy director of the Children's Museum Pittsburgh and currently deputy director at the Parrish Art Museum, describes some ways that he considers outcomes and impacts internally and externally, as well as lessons from the Children's Museum Pittsburgh's approach and process. Siefert notes that an important component of community work is understanding the political dynamic, becoming politically savvy, and learning how to effectively work with people who are within that dynamic:

> An example is a unique project launched by the Children's Museum called the UNDERPASS project, where an outdoor public art gallery was created. There are three underpasses (railroad bridges) for entering the neighborhood, and all three of them are in a state of disrepair. For pedestrians in particular, there is water leaking through the bridges, the lighting is bad, and the sidewalks are crumbling. An agreement was reached whereby the Community Development Corporation (CDC) would lead the development and raise the money to improve two of the three, and the third one would be left to the cultural sector. Even though the CDC and the Children's Museum had the same goals – to improve the safety and security of the underpasses – it was better to have separate projects, to draw a line and say, "OK, that's your project and this is our project."
>
> For museum leaders to foster a stronger culture of community based work, it's important for them to internally reflect on what their own aspirations are, what some of their objectives might be over the next three to five years. It's like a strategic planning process where one works on understanding what one's strengths and weaknesses are, and how one might position that towards a community engagement process. Find opportunities to reflect internally and assess objectives and look at work that is probably already going on to help shape strategies. From that, one can get into a broader inquiry with staff and board, and neighbors or schools. This leads naturally to identifying who you think you can work with and where the opportunities are. We see the museum's staff as *conveners*, not necessarily the *leaders*, in this process. Inquiry-based meetings will naturally start where leaders are asking questions and listening to others talking about agendas. Hopefully they will share some things about their agenda, and then *they* begin to think internally about whether or not there's opportunity for collaboration. It's hard to explain in a linear fashion, because it's not a linear process, but there's definitely this moment that people face, internally, of "Do we even need to do this? What are our objectives?" Leaders and community people become more comfortable talking with each other about what it is they are actually interested in trying to do.
>
> One reason one might start to do that first step – initiate community work—is that someone in the organization sees something already happening. Those might be little things, but there's something already going on.

They recognize that they are already putting resources toward this. And they are on their way.

C. Siefert, personal communication, May 2, 2016

Siefert's comments about the political dynamic raise important points about the complexities of community involvement. Understanding how things get done in a community, through official or governmental channels and through community-based leadership, is an essential aspect of knowing who needs to be involved and on board. Governmental agencies have their own roles and responsibilities in serving communities, and they are essential partners in the community-building process. Understanding the most effective ways to work with governmental agencies is a key component of successful community-building efforts.

Siefert acknowledges the importance of internal planning and that planning helps foster a culture of community-focused work. Siefert's perspective reveals many of the attributes of community-focused institutions discussed in Chapter 6. Some of the questions about readiness that were posed in Chapter 6 are relevant here – they illustrate what readiness looks like in this brief example:

- Q: What *indicators* – signposts that reveal readiness to share authority – are in place?
  A: The UNDERPASS project is an example of shared authority. Overall, the museum sees itself as a convener, not necessarily the leader, in this process.
- Q: How do the museum's leadership and staff *demonstrate* readiness to share authority? What internal and external processes are in place to support this readiness?
  A: The planning process and inquiry-based meetings, which provide the space and opportunity to think about collaboration in a thoughtful, comfortable way.

Other examples from the Children's Museum Pittsburgh highlight the ways in which a culture of community-focused work is embedded and how it considers outcomes and impacts internally and externally.

The Charm Bracelet Project has been another community-wide project that involves the Children's Museum Pittsburgh. Pittsburgh's North Side, the museum's neighborhood, had been in decline for a number of years. When the museum was renovated in 2004, providing greatly expanded space, museum staff recognized the desire and need to connect more fully with other community organizations to stimulate and bring about positive change in the neighborhood. The intention was to have cultural organizations serve as active participants ("charms") in building a healthier community and strengthening connections among community organizations and assets. The "bracelet" is composed of links or programs throughout the neighborhood, with the intention of revitalizing the North Side and its residents. Participating organizations include the Children's Museum Pittsburgh, which provided space for community organizations that work with or on behalf of children;

New Hazlett Theater, which was renovated and reactivated to provide performance space for the community; National Aviary; Mattress Factory Contemporary Art Museum; Carnegie Library; Carnegie Science Center; Andy Warhol Museum; Artists Image Resource; Cities of Asylum; Manchester Craftsmen's Guild; Saturday Light Brigade; and Venture Outdoors.

For the Children's Museum, one of the outcomes has been the establishment of strong relationships with on-site partners. The museum's renovation in 2004 greatly expanded its space, and with a belief in the importance of being a community anchor, the museum shared that space with community organizations that work with or on behalf of children. This enabled relationships to grow and deepen, and the ability to share space meant the ability to share ideas, sparking new collaborative projects to serve the community. As the museum notes,

> The abiding goal was to make a more unified cultural district on the North Side. Perhaps the best result was that the new construction had reinforced the Children's Museum's reputation as an agent for positive change in its community.
>
> The tangible results of the Charm Bracelet Project include dozens of collaborative programs, special projects, large scale initiatives and newfound alliances that in total reflect shared purposes and make unpredictable connections. These demonstrate a deepening commitment to the neighborhood by all of its residents and bolster the sense of camaraderie that has developed among the participants. Increasingly, a sense of unity characterizes the project initiatives, because amid the diversity lies a common enfranchisement that contributes palpably to a shared identity of the whole.
>
> *Children's Museum Pittsburgh, 2013*

The leadership and staff of the Children's Museum Pittsburgh reflect on the impacts of extensive relationships and a higher degree of trust among community members. Jane Werner, executive director of the Children's Museum Pittsburgh, shares her perspective about outcomes and creating a stronger culture of community internally:

> We can look at the number of people using the park as a measurable outcome. It was never used before, and now it is used a great deal. In addition, the theater is thriving – people are using it – you can see it – you can feel it. We are a site of community meetings. People are comfortable here. We say "yes" to almost everything. "Sure, why not?" is our attitude. We do measure things, and our Department of Research and Learning is deeply involved in the museum's programs – we build research into the design of all of our projects.
>
> At the Children's Museum, we are known as a place you can kick off your shoes and learn something. We want great architecture and design for people to feel at ease. I love coming to work – we laugh a lot! We have grown from a small institution to a mid-size museum, and there has been a cultural shift. Fifteen years ago we were a staff of 25, and now we have 55 full time and

150 part time staff members. We are trying to hang onto the mom and pop culture of "Let's try it!" and it can be a challenge. Communication is incredibly important. We have a communications task force to help make sure we are as welcoming to our staff as we are to our visitors. We have a good sense of humor and a dynamic management team.

One of the ways that we create and nurture a strong culture of community internally is placing conversation between our staff and our visitors at the core of the museum experience. We try to create points of discussion in a safe place. I would encourage museum leaders to walk around their institutions often, focusing on connecting with people. You have to be present. Know and trust the folks around you. Say "yes!" even if it is a crazy idea, and be OK with failing. Build up your resources and financial cushions, so that you are able to say "Yes!" and to be a true part of the community.

J. Werner, personal communication, May 17, 2016

These stories from the Children's Museum Pittsburgh reveal a number of attributes and strategies that are important in museum–community involvement. They include the importance of face-to-face interaction, sharing authority, valuing and respecting what every person and organization brings to the table, humility, patience and tenacity, the ability to listen, seeking to learn, flexibility, resiliency, and empathy. These attributes and strategies inform the Children's Museum Pittsburgh as it considers its impact in the community.

Another way of assessing the impact on the museum and in the community is to look at how a community organizing process changes internal practice. Hiring and supporting staff with community-focused skills and attributes can help facilitate this. When these skills and attributes – including listening, empathy, and community organizing – become part of the internal culture of an organization, the impacts can be significant.

Stories from the Field: Queens Museum

The Queens Museum, located in Flushing Meadows Corona Park in New York City, sees the impacts of long-term community work in profound ways. Some years ago the museum realized the importance of focusing on the Corona neighborhood to help revitalize it. Prerana Reddy, director of Public Programs & Community Engagement at the Queens Museum, notes:

When the department was just started in 2004, in our conversations with many people at community organizations, we asked if their constituencies would be interested in community arts. We found out where the community interests lay and where the museum could do something. In the Corona neighborhood, especially, we asked community members what issues are of concern, and they told us that education, immigration issues, and language access issues are big concerns. We were able to do this (have these conversations) effectively because one of our staff members worked for the US Census as an immigration outreach specialist before coming to work at the museum.

Our first community organizer, hired in 2006, had worked on political campaigns for a local elected official, and already had a good knowledge of the community and how to go door-to-door to connect with people. It's important to hire people who already have these types of experiences. They come with a strong set of skills, as well as contacts and a rolodex. We started with the people we (and she) knew and worked from there. We set up a meeting with community leaders and said, "We'd like to be good neighbors." Community members came with a laundry list of wants. We considered these, and decided what we could start with. This led to our work developing Corona Plaza and doing artist residencies there in conjunction with our plaza festivals. After doing an evaluation of that first residency, we realized that longer-term engagement, the ability to speak the dominant language (Spanish), and a more open-ended way of working were called for. This led us to Corona Studio – the neighborhood itself could be a studio for artists who wanted to research and address social issues. The first of these was Immigrant Movement International initiated by Cuban artist Tania Bruguera in 2011.

The community wanted a space for learning, artmaking, and activism in their neighborhood, and Immigrant Movement International filled this role in its storefront office. A dedicated set of users of the space had developed in the first two years that Bruguera led the project with input from Queens Museum staff. When Bruguera moved on, these users wanted to continue the project and the Museum agreed to support them financially, strategically, and administratively. A community council comprised of those who used the space and Museum staff was created to collaboratively make decisions. Public action emerging from the community and now community members are developing the space. We started by saying, "What are people saying they need, and how can we address this?" This work is revitalizing the neighbor-hood, and the indicators we see are in the public space projects, such as Corona Plaza, where we created a community process to design and program a once-derelict parking lot into a vibrant public plaza. We commissioned urban planners and designers to communicate the residents' ideas to the Department of Transportation which was overseeing the project. We also worked to find local artists and performers interested in programming, and helped find a maintenance partner. This is one of the earliest non-Manhattan groups to do it. The city's maintenance requirements made it difficult for lower income neighborhoods, those that didn't already have Business Improvement Districts, to accomplish. It highlights the museum's advocacy role and shows other neighborhoods what it is possible to do with strategic partnerships and community buy-in.

We are continuing to engage people in public space issues. We've been part of coalitions that have been fighting the encroachment of private

FIGURE 10.1 Queens Museum: Immigrant Movement International

development and events in Flushing Meadows in Corona Park, where the Museum is located. Corona Park already houses professional baseball and tennis stadiums. This activism resulted in a new nonprofit alliance forming, to support the improvement of Flushing Meadows Corona Park. To prepare residents to participate in the Alliance's Community Advisory Board, we worked with Design Trust for Public Space to create a community design school in which local residents learn about the biggest concerns of both the parks administration *and* park-goers, and how the park's capital processes work. It's a 10-week course that is building capacity for ordinary citizens to do their own research and prototyping, and present the best proposals to the Alliance and Parks Department for funding and implementation.

We hope to build on previous projects. We are looking at institutional changes, not just in our department (Public Programs & Community Engagement) but in other departments, as well, such as curatorial and education. Over time, staff members throughout the institution have developed a sense of pride that they have an identity and reputation for innovation and social purpose, that they have a vision and set of ethics to guide their programming. Over time, when people see that things work and how the public responds, they see that these changes are good for the Museum.

These projects work because we are already working with community members and organizations on an ongoing basis. We already have relationships in place, and we are able to see how a project fits into a longer term neighborhood change goal.

P. Reddy, personal communication, October 1, 2015

As described by Reddy, the Queens Museum's long-term work with the community is having many impacts, within the organization, in its community, and more broadly. A recurrent theme, both explicitly and implicitly stated, is that of wanting to be a good neighbor. This plays out in a number of ways, from listening in community conversations and learning what the museum could do, to creating training opportunities for local residents, where they learn about how to work with park-goers and the parks administration – building neighborhood capacity in the process.

It is clear when listening to Reddy that the impacts are far-reaching. The Queens Museum's programming reflects what they learn in the community about the importance of language access and a focus on immigration issues. Internally, the leadership and staff have a sense of pride that what the institution is doing is making a difference. Within the community, the impacts of each initiative build on others. The Immigrant Movement International project is continuing with museum support, the neighborhoods are being revitalized, and the museum is supporting a community design school with the intent to build capacity. What is notable is that all these efforts demonstrate to other neighborhoods what can happen with strategic partnerships and with people who believe in and will fully participate in revitalizing their neighborhoods. Each project can be analyzed to assess the outcomes and impacts of the individual project, and collectively they provide a picture of an organization that is working with its community to effect change.

The detailed stories from the Children's Museum Pittsburgh and the Queens Museum describe how extensive community work leads to long-term outcomes and impacts in community change efforts. The National Endowment for the Arts, recognizing the importance of bringing together health, research, and the arts, has published a useful guide for those in the health and arts sectors. *The National Endowment for the Arts Guide to Community-Engaged Research in the Arts and Health* provides guidance on how to partner effectively to document and assess how community-based arts programs are associated with positive health outcomes. This guide is particularly useful for museums and cultural organizations as they consider outcomes of their community-focused work. What is particularly notable is its section on how to develop research questions and how to identify and select outcome measures. Authors Jeffrey Chapline, founder of New Art Horizons, and Julene K. Johnson, professor and associate director at the UCSF Institute for Health & Aging and Center for Aging in Diverse Communities, discuss the difference between and uses for both scientific research and program evaluation. They describe community-engaged research and the uses for qualitative and quantitative research methods, how to find research partners, and how to document your programs.

Accountability

Desirable outcomes and impacts are much more likely to occur when there is accountability. Creating guidelines, policies, and strategic and action plans for inclusion and community involvement are important and necessary tasks. Such things will be effective only when museum and community leadership hold responsible people accountable for their actions. This is systemic change in the way museums operate. Programs and policy statements are important aspects of this, but it is only through holding organizations accountable for community involvement and inclusive practices that organizations will be community focused and inclusive.

The institution will need to answer the following questions: How will the museum and community leadership define institutional accountability? What is the institutional will to commit resources and build capacity? What are the minimum standards and metrics for measuring ongoing progress? This does not mean checking off boxes ("We did these community-based programs this year, which were attended by this number of people. We developed a policy statement on the value of inclusion."). Does the museum include specific responsibilities for community involvement in each position description? At annual performance reviews, is community involvement included as part of each staff member's goal setting, ensuring that staff members work to achieve these community involvement goals?

One example of accountability is told by Eric Jolly, former CEO of the Science Museum of Minnesota (now president and CEO of Minnesota Philanthropy Partners), who related the following during the *Diversity: From Talk to Action* session at the American Alliance of Museums annual meeting in May 2016:

> In one institution, I had a very simple rule. You had to have at least one qualified minority candidate in your finalist pool, to prove to me that you did an adequate search. And then you could interview. And if, when you finished interviewing, you didn't hire that qualified minority you had found, you had to write the non-select reason. [It's easy to say] why it's *good* to hire someone – "Oh, I hired them because . . ." I want to know, "Why did you tell me that person was qualified, and then pass on them?" In my experience, very few people ever wanted to write that letter twice. And if you did write that letter twice, you risked losing hiring authority and it got bumped up from the department to the deanship. And if the dean failed twice, it got bumped up from the dean to the vice president. It never got bumped to me. That was good. Changing policy can change the system.
>
> Changing programs can change the system. In one institution we put together a youth science group that was stunning. And we trained them up in how to work in every aspect of the museum in every language that they spoke. And we created a cadre of young people who were ready to take leadership positions. In another we created fellowship programs that last three years, and place upcoming people with ambition in a leadership program to

work in three different positions in the institution side by side with other professionals, knowing they had a three-year commitment. So far, every one of those people have been offered a job of permanence within one year. Policy – you can change it. Program – you can do it.

And it's got to also be personal. I remember the day I was at Taco Bell. I love Taco Bell. And I was greeted by the most enthusiastic person I have ever seen. He was working hard; he was cheerful; he was the face of the future that I wanted to imagine we will all live in. And I gave that young man my business card. And on the back was a note that said, "This guarantees an informational interview for you at my museum." And I said, "Call this number" and it was the HR Director. And every time I personally gave out one of those cards, we hired a young person, away from Taco Bell, to a living wage and a career pathway that started as our public face. There's more that we can do. We can offer to change the way in which we do job descriptions, to list cultural competency. We keep a blog in our institution, and you can look up definitions of cultural competency, but some of them include second language abilities, some of them include international experience, or experience with international communities in our own town. And we consider that a plus to a hiring, that means as much [as] your educational attainment. You can change those policies. You can actually pay someone more for speaking a second language if they're willing to do it at work. Try it! It changes the value of that, in your community.

Now, if you do all of those things, if you work on the personal level, if you work on the program level and you work on the policy level, and you bring in a cadre of people, you have to worry about keeping them. And that's a tough one. We very often work at keeping them in a way that we don't fully understand its broader impact. It wears them down. I was at a university once, doing some research in which we looked at the value of their faculty across interdepartmental committees, and we did something called the Monte Carlo study, where we randomly sampled the demographic qualifications of every faculty member as if they were randomly assigned to a committee. We did it again, and again, and again, and by accident, by chance, if you did that with this particular institution, there would have been seven committees that were of majority-minority people, and there would have been five that were 100% women. But there was only one at that institution that was 100% women. Any guess? It was women's studies, because why should men know? Odd, huh? And there were none that were 100% or even a majority of minority people, because the institution had a very egalitarian rule. They wanted to have a woman or a minority or a person with disability on every committee, thus absolutely statistically guaranteeing that every committee would have a majority of majority people. It's what we call the opportunity for input without the opportunity for impact. That's my definition of tokenism. We have to allow communities to write their own agenda. And so there are three critical questions that we ask:

- Who informs the work? Who sets the agenda? Who asks the question? Who identified the product that you need? If you go to the Gila River reservation in Arizona, virtually 100% of the men age 35 and older will have diabetes. Their average life expectancy? Just a few years shy of the onset of Alzheimer's. If you ask this community where they want to put their public health research dollars, they're going to tell you they'd like to live long enough to worry about Alzheimer's. There's nothing wrong with doing Alzheimer's research, but recognize that when you change who informs the work, you get a different agenda. You get a different priority. You get things rising to the surface you may have never considered.

- Who forms the work? Who actually constructs the piece? If you don't change that, the piece will be irrelevant. In the wonderful state of Minnesota, we give every four year old a language readiness test. And that test was written by a place almost as diverse as Minnesota – Iowa. The language readiness test requires four year olds to differentiate between nonsense syllables and real words. And I live in the state with the largest Hmong population in the world. Five of the nonsense syllables identified in that Iowa test are complete words in the Hmong language. Children who are bilingual were listed as lower literacy rates than those who only spoke one language, because who *formed* the work was not as diverse as those who experience the work. Who forms, informs, and who benefits from the work – we have always measured that one. How many minorities walk through our door? Well, how many minorities wrote the story and told you what they wanted to see? When we change that, we change our exhibits. At the Science Museum [of Minnesota], we courageously launched an exhibit on race. And I know it was a good exhibit because we got enough death threats to make the exhibit credible, but not enough credible death threats to make it dangerous. And it took a staff that was willing to listen to someone other than themselves, to have a different community set the agenda, and to measure who benefits in different ways than who pays gate. And when we did that, we made magic.

Jolly, 2016, May

Eric Jolly's example of accountability is courageous and achievable and shows how changing one internal process yields significant results. Jolly poses important questions about who informs the work and sets the agenda and who has hiring authority. Through putting simple yet effective mechanisms in place for making hiring decisions, the internal culture says, "We are here for all."

Another example of accountability is demonstrated by the City of New York/Office of Cultural Affairs in its July 2017 publication *CreateNYC: A Cultural Plan for All New Yorkers*. The City of New York funds almost a thousand cultural organizations each year. In a press conference to announce the plan, Mayor Bill de Blasio and Commissioner for Cultural Affairs Tom Finkelpearl talked about the importance of being inclusive and that focus underpins this cultural plan. They identified three specific steps that are being taken: The city will collect information on the demographic makeup of the boards and staffs of cultural organizations. The organizations that request city funding will be asked to provide their vision on how they address equity and inclusion and to provide a diversity and inclusion plan – with measurable goals – for their staffs and boards. The answers that the cultural organizations provide to these questions will be a factor in city funding going forward (NYC Mayor's Office, 2017).

What is especially notable is that the City of New York is clearly saying to cultural organizations, "You will be accountable for this – setting measurable goals for inclusion is a factor in making decisions about city funding." Organizations will need to have a diversity and inclusion plan in order to receive city funding. Accountability does not stop there – the city is providing trainings to assist cultural organizations in addressing the grant guidelines, thus helping organizations understand what they need to include in their diversity and inclusion plan as well as how to set diversity and inclusion goals and develop an inclusion plan.

Both of the examples noted above focus on accountability in terms of who is serving on the staff and who is serving on the board. Examples of diversity are more easily measured (through demographic analysis) than other examples of inclusion, and accountability is tied to measurability. Earlier in this chapter when outcomes and impacts were discussed, a number of questions were posed to assist the reader in determining whether and how to set measurable goals. Accountability can also be built into systems, such as annual staff performance reviews and goal setting, where each staff member's work in community and inclusion over the year is measured according to goals and expectations set the prior year. Organizations such as the Oakland Museum of California use this form of accountability, and it is one way to build accountability into regular museum operations.

A useful tool to assist in creating metrics is the Empathetic Museum Maturity Model, described as *A Metric for Institutional Transformation*:

> Empathy is valued as an individual trait – an ability to emotionally connect with another person and value their life experience in an authentic way. But what about our cultural institutions? At a time when "diversity" and "inclusion" are more critical than ever to the future of our field, how can institutions themselves better reflect and represent the values of their communities?

> **This assessment tool is proposed to help organizations move towards a more empathetic future.**

> *CHARACTERISTICS*
> These categories were defined to capture the wide variety of ways that empathy can be reflected within and by an institution. Civic Vision, Institutional Body Language, and Community Resonance relate to institutional identity and

relationships, both internal and external. Timeliness & Sustainability and Performance Measures focus more on operational functions and assessment.

Empathetic Museum Maturity Model: A Metric
for Institutional Transformation, n.d.

The model is in the form of a rubric and asks questions such as, "How does the museum value, relate to, and serve its diverse communities?" According to the model, the qualities that one would look for include "Persistent awareness of surrounding community; forges strong, trusted connections with all (often underrepresented) segments of community in terms of race, ethnicity, gender, sexual orientation, disability, socioeconomic status." Organizations utilizing this rubric may look internally at their culture and practice and use this rubric to guide discussion on where they are in each characteristic – from lowest maturity level to advanced maturity level.

Considering and planning for outcomes, impacts, and accountability is core to designing any museum–community work and to truly embedding this is into one's institution. As noted at the beginning of this chapter, museum leadership and staff will need to think about how to assess impacts and to consider how they will know when their organization is truly involved with its community.

Looking to the Future

I am convinced that concrete action starts with small changes which can burgeon into quite widespread new beginnings.

Elaine Heumann Gurian, Intentional Civility

The vision of museums and cultural organizations as vital members of their communities is slowly becoming a reality for more organizations, especially those that embrace the community wholeheartedly. These lessons and stories illustrate how it looks and feels to be involved with one's community and to have one's community be involved with one's organization. This book has provided the foundation for understanding community involvement, examples and stories that illustrate different types of museums involved with their communities, and the tools that will help foster the skills and attributes of this work. Collectively, they will guide museum leadership and staff as they develop, nurture, and deepen museum–community involvement.

These stories reflect a strong and abiding commitment to this work. It is not just how these organizations do business – it is how they *are*. It is embedded in every aspect of their organizational culture. The stories' intent is to illustrate, in clear and vibrant ways, what museum and community involvement looks like in practice.

Museum–community involvement is a continuum. A museum, its leadership, and its staff may be at different points of this continuum simultaneously. In looking to the future, the fervent hope is that every person and every organization continues to move along that continuum, to be more fully and authentically involved in one's community and to more fully and authentically involve the community in the museum.

Bibliography

Chapline, J., & Johnson, J. (2016, December). *The National Endowment for the Arts guide to community-engaged research in the arts and health*. Retrieved from https://www.arts.gov/sites/default/files/Guide-to-Community-Engaged-Research-in-the-Arts-and-Health-March2017.pdf

Children's Museum Pittsburgh. (2013). *Charm Bracelet Project: Culture and community on Pittsburgh's North Side*. Pittsburgh: Children's Museum Pittsburgh and ETC Press.

City of New York. (2017, July). *CreateNYC: A cultural plan for all New Yorkers*. Retrieved from http://createnyc.org/wp-content/uploads/2017/07/CreateNYC_Report_FIN.pdf

Empathetic museum maturity model: A metric for institutional transformation. (n.d.). Retrieved from http://empatheticmuseum.weebly.com/maturity-model.html

Frechtling Westat, J., Frierson, H., Hood, S., & Hughes, G. (2002). *The 2002 user-friendly handbook for project evaluation*. Washington, DC: The National Science Foundation. Retrieved from https://www.nsf.gov/pubs/2002/nsf02057/nsf02057.pdf

Gurian, E. H. (2014, October). Intentional civility. *Curator: The Museum Journal, 57*(4), 473–484.

Jolly, E. (2016, May). *Diversity: From talk to action*. Session conducted at the annual meeting of the American Alliance of Museums, Washington, DC.

Matthew, K. (2017, February 10). Community catalyst: How do we know we are having an impact? [Blog post]. Retrieved from https://www.imls.gov/news-events/upnext-blog/2017/02/community-catalyst-how-do-we-know-we-are-having-impact

Norton, M., & Dowdall, E. (2017, January). *Strengthening networks, sparking change: Museums and libraries as community catalysts 2016*. Washington, DC: Institute of Museum and Library Services. Retrieved from https://www.imls.gov/sites/default/files/publications/documents/community-catalyst-report-january-2017.pdf

NYC Mayor's Office. (2017, July 19). *Mayor de Blasio holds media availability to announce CreateNYC* [Video file]. Retrieved from https://www.youtube.com/watch?v=A6zkRQKXI4w

Appendix A
SAMPLE FORMS, LETTERS, AND WORKSHEETS

1. Community Research Update Form and Online Research Form
   These forms will help you to record and keep track of all your community research efforts. Share them with other people on your team so you can all benefit from the research. This information will be useful when you create your Community Profile.

2. Connecting with Community Members: Sample Email Letters
   Examples of initial letters to community members whom one may or may not know.

3. Example of Interview Questions
   Example of potential interview questions for key stakeholders.

4. Community Involvement Action Plan Year _____ to Year _____
   Useful format to use in creating the action plan.

5. Community Involvement Action Plan Timeline Year _____ to Year _____
   Useful format to use in creating the action plan timeline; similar to the information above but laid out chronologically.

6. Community Involvement Master Contact List
   Useful form to collect and consolidate all relevant information about contacts. The intent of this form is to share it with other people in your organization so that each person has access to relevant information. For example, perhaps someone in the Education Department has done a joint program with another organization. Perhaps the director of the museum is interested in learning more about the organization and can utilize the information in this document to get started.

Community Research Update Form

This form will help you to record and keep track of all your community research efforts. Share it with other people on your team so you can all benefit from the research. This information will be useful when you create your Community Profile.

Date	Who you contacted *Include how you contacted them (Phone? Email? In person? Visited their organization?)*	Where you visited (real places)	Online resources you visited	Result *Did the person you contacted get back to you?*	Follow-up needed *Ideas for what you will do to follow up*	Follow-up done *Include date accomplished*

Online Research Form

This form will help you to record and keep track of what you learn online. Share it with other people on your team so you can all benefit from the research. This information will be useful when you create your Community Profile.

Date	Name of website and link to site	Keywords	Level of importance for reference (1–5; 5 = info we need at our fingertips)	Main takeaways

Connecting with Community Members: Sample Email Letters

Sample email letter to someone you know whom you called but didn't have a chance to talk to directly

Dear _____,

Thanks so much for returning my call on Friday. Sorry I missed you!

I called because I'm working on a project that I thought might be of interest to you. The _____ Museum is developing an exhibition and programs on _____. The museum is putting together a community advisory committee of people who are active in the _____ community who might be interested in giving suggestions for programs, reviewing label copy, and assisting in publicizing the exhibition. The museum staff is very interested in ensuring that the exhibition is relevant and accessible and in building relationships with community leaders. As we were suggesting people to be part of the committee, I thought of you, and I would consider it an honor if you would be part of this advisory committee. We will meet three times and do the rest of the work via email. Here's what we hope the community advisory committee members will do:

- Review label copy
- Assist in recommending programs to go along with the exhibition
- Publicize the exhibit and programs
- Encourage organizations to plan group visits to the exhibition
- Assist in recommending and/or recruiting docents
- Assist with providing the names of people and groups to contact to publicize the exhibition and programs.

We do have a small honorarium to offer advisory committee members. We will be meeting on Tuesday, March 26, from 6:00–7:30 p.m. at the museum, and I would love to have you be part of this committee. Sound interesting? I hope so!

I am attaching a brief description of the exhibition so you can see why we're excited about this.

Please let me know what you think. I hope you say yes!

Sincerely,

Sample email letter to someone you don't know whom you identified by looking up a contact name on an organization's website

Dear _____,

Sorry I missed you when I called this morning.

I called because I wanted to introduce myself and because I'm working on a project that I thought might be of interest to you. The _____ Museum is developing an exhibition and programs on _____. The museum is putting together a community advisory committee of people who are active in the _____ community who might be interested in giving suggestions for programs, reviewing label copy, and assisting in publicizing the exhibition. The museum staff is very interested in ensuring that the exhibition is relevant and accessible and in building relationships with community leaders. As we were thinking of people to be part of the committee, I thought of you because of your leadership of the _____. We would consider it an honor if you would be part of this advisory committee. We will meet three times and do the rest of the work via email. Here's what we hope the community advisory committee members will do:

- Review label copy
- Assist in recommending programs to go along with the exhibition
- Publicize the exhibit and programs
- Encourage organizations to plan group visits to the exhibition
- Assist in recommending and/or recruiting docents
- Assist with providing the names of people and groups to contact to publicize the exhibition and programs.

We do have a small honorarium to offer advisory committee members. We will be meeting on Tuesday, March 26, from 6:00–7:30 p.m. at the museum, and we would love to have you be part of this committee. Sound interesting? I hope so! I am attaching a brief description of the exhibition so you can see why we're excited about this.

Please let me know what you think. I hope you say yes!

Sincerely,

Sample email letter to people you don't know who were referred to you

Dear _____,

_____ recommended that I contact you about an upcoming project at the _____ Museum. The museum is developing an exhibition and programs on _____. The museum is putting together a community advisory committee of people who are active in the _____ community who might be interested in giving suggestions for programs, reviewing label copy, and assisting in publicizing the exhibition. The museum staff is very interested in ensuring that the exhibition is relevant and accessible and in building relationships with community leaders. As I mentioned, _____ recommended that you would be great for this because of your work in the _____ and your knowledge _____. We would consider it an honor for you to be part of this advisory committee. We will meet three times and do the rest of the work via email. Here's what we hope the community advisory committee members will do:

– Review label copy
– Assist in recommending programs to go along with the exhibition
– Publicize the exhibit and programs
– Encourage organizations to plan group visits to the exhibition
– Assist in recommending and/or recruiting docents
– Assist with providing the names of people and groups to contact to publicize the exhibition and programs.

We do have a small honorarium to offer advisory committee members. We will be meeting on Tuesday, March 26, from 6:00–7:30 p.m. at the museum, and we would love to have you be part of this committee. Sound interesting? I hope so! I am attaching a brief description of the exhibition so you can see why we're excited about this.

Please let me know what you think. I hope you say yes!

Sincerely,

_____ **Museum**
Potential Interview Questions for Key Stakeholders (Example)

Name of interviewee:
Organization:
Address:
Phone:
Email:
Date interview conducted:
Interviewer:

---

1. Please describe the mission of your organization and its programs and services. [Note: I have read through your website, so I'm interested in your perspectives and work that might not be included there.]

2. What are the top three issues and trends that you will need to address in your work in the next one to three years? How do you anticipate addressing them?

3. What is your current work relationship with the _____ Museum? Can you give us a brief history of how that relationship developed?

4. What do you consider to be the unique and distinctive characteristics of the ___ Museum?

5. In your opinion, what barriers might prevent people from visiting the _____ Museum?

6. How do you see developing and strengthening your joint work with the museum?

7. What advice and suggestions would you give to the _____ Museum so that its work assists your own?

8. Is there anyone else whom we should talk to?

Community Involvement Action Plan Year _____ – Year _____

Organization's Mission

Goals	Detailed strategies / actions	Who is responsible?	Resources needed ($/ people)	Timeframe	Evaluation strategies	Potential outcomes
1. [Program area (e.g., marketing)]						
1.1	1.1.1					
	1.1.2					
	1.1.3					
1.2	1.2.1					
	1.2.2					
	1.2.3					
	1.2.4					

Community Involvement Action Plan Timeline Year _____ – Year _____

Program area	Detailed strategies/actions	Year 1 Months 1–3 (e.g., Jan–March)	Year 1 Months 4–6 (e.g., April–June)	Year 1 Months 7–9 (e.g., July–Sept)	Year 1 Months 10–12 (e.g., Oct–Dec)	Year 2 Months 1–6 (e.g., Jan–June)	Year 2 Months 7–12 (e.g., July–Dec)	Year 3 (e.g., Jan–Dec)

Community Involvement Master Contact List

Name and title/ role of person contacted	Organization	Contact info	Brief description of organization, including primary audiences served	Key points from your conversation, including your name and the date you contacted them	Recommended follow-up actions and who will/ could do them	Date follow-up actions done	Additional ideas for engaging this person/ organization (include your name and the date with each idea)	Donor potential? (yes/no)

Appendix B
ACTIVITIES: WORKING TOGETHER

The Name Game: Getting to Know One Another

Often, when people work together internally (within their organizations), they know only a limited amount about one another. The Name Game is an opportunity for people who work together to share more about themselves in a safe environment. Each person determines what they want to share.

The activity: Each person talks about their name(s). They can share whatever they want about their name. Here are some prompting questions, and each person can share as much or as little as they want: Were you named after someone else? Has your name ever changed? What led to the change? Has your name changed from previous generations? If so, why was it changed? Does your name have a specific meaning? Why were you given the name you were? Have you ever had a nickname? Who calls (or called) you by your nickname? Do you like that name? This is the time that each person can share whatever stories they wish about their name, including how it is pronounced.

This activity is best done early in the process of working together as a team and getting to know one another, and it is an example of how we can build trust and learn about one another. The lessons learned from the Name Game are:

- Take the time to learn about the people you work with and those you might want to establish a relationship with.
- Don't make assumptions about a person or group of people.
- There's more to a person than what you see.

Respect is a core value and a key component of museum–community involvement, and you will practice it internally and externally. Focus on the importance of listening fully, paying attention, and being respectful in your community work, and that includes the internal community of your organization.

Teamwork

You will often work in teams for collaborative projects.

   The activity: Brainstorm about teamwork.

- What are all the things you like about working on a team? Write them down so everyone can see them.
- What are all the things you don't like about working on a team? Write them down so everyone can see them.
- How can you maximize the things you like about working on teams?
- How can you minimize the things you don't like about working on teams?

In your teams, review the lists you created above, and use the following tips to bring your team together. Internally, your staff is also a team, so these guidelines apply to your interactions with other staff members and with the community members. Be respectful and demonstrate integrity.

Working in Teams: A Few Useful Tips for Getting Organized and Staying on Track

1. *Determine roles*: Discuss what role each team member can play and how you will collectively make decisions. Determine whether someone will take on the role of project manager to help keep everyone on track. Also, determine how you will communicate and share information.
2. *Set ground rules*: Determine and set basic ground rules for how you will work together. They may include being prepared for meetings (reading the materials and completing the tasks you have agreed to), being on time for meetings, keeping notes, being respectful, listening clearly and with an open mind, providing everyone a chance to talk, and summarizing decisions and next steps before you leave.
3. *Define the goal for the project*: Be as specific as you can.
4. *List tasks to be completed*: Be somewhat detailed so you can see everything that needs to be done. Perhaps one of your teammates is an organized thinker, so this might be one of their contributions.
5. *Assign responsibility for all tasks*: Tasks should be divided so all members receive an equitable number of tasks. Check to see that all team members are satisfied with the tasks they have been assigned.
6. *Develop a timeline and checklist*: Things often take longer than you antici-pate, so build some flexibility into the timeline. Make sure that everyone agrees to the timeline. Share it among all team members (per your communication agreement in #1).
7. *Share team meeting notes*: Make sure that you post your team meeting notes per your communication agreement in #1. This helps clarify team agreements and deadlines.

INDEX

Page numbers in *italics* denote figures.